The Shadow of Death

The Shadow of Death

The Holocaust in Lithuania

Harry Gordon

THE UNIVERSITY PRESS OF KENTUCKY

Copyright © 1992 by The University Press of Kentucky

Scholarly publisher for the Commonwealth,
serving Bellarmine University, Berea College, Centre
College of Kentucky, Eastern Kentucky University,
The Filson Historical Society, Georgetown College,
Kentucky Historical Society, Kentucky State University,
Morehead State University, Murray State University,
Northern Kentucky University, Transylvania University,
University of Kentucky, University of Louisville,
and Western Kentucky University.
All rights reserved.

Editorial and Sales Offices: The University Press of Kentucky
663 South Limestone Street, Lexington, Kentucky 40508-4008
www.kentuckypress.com

Library of Congress Cataloging-in-Publication Data

Gordon, Harry, 1925–
    The shadow of death : The Holocaust in Lithuania / Harry Gordon
    p.   cm.
    ISBN-10: 0-8131-1767-4 (acid-free) ; ISBN-10: 0-8131-9008-8 (pbk.)
    1. Jews—Lithuania—Kaunas—Persecutions. 2. Holocaust, Jewish
(1939–1945)—Lithuania—Kaunas—Personal narratives. 3. Gordon,
Harry, 1925–   4. Kaunas (Lithuania)—Ethnic relations. I. Title.
DS135.R93K2835   1992
940.53'18'09475—dc20   91-23548
ISBN-13: 978-0-8131-9008-2 (pbk. : alk. paper)

This book is printed on acid-free recycled paper meeting
the requirements of the American National Standard
for Permanence in Paper for Printed Library Materials.

Manufactured in the United States of America.

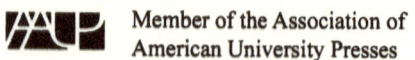

In memory of my mother, father, aunts, uncles, and cousins
who perished in the Holocaust;
and for my children, Eric, Abraham, and Vivian,
and my grandchildren—
so they will know their own history

Contents

Foreword by Theodore S. Hamerow ix
Acknowledgments xvii
1. Before the War 1
2. The Russian Invasion 9
3. The War Begins 22
4. The Purge of Slobodka 37
5. Moving to the Ghetto 41
6. In the Ghetto 43
7. The Collection of Valuables 46
8. The First Practice Massacre 50
9. The Airfield Work Brigade 55
10. The Liquidation of the Little Ghetto 59
11. Life in the Big Ghetto 63
12. The Big Liquidation 65
13. The Workshops and the Small Brigades 69
14. The Jewish Police 73
15. New Life and New Work 75
16. Koshedar 88
17. Back in the Ghetto 99
18. Escape from the Ghetto 106
19. A New Work Brigade 115
20. Red Plantation 118
21. The *Obersturmbannführer* 122
22. The Liquidation of the Helpless 126
23. The Partisans in the Woods 131
24. Kazlu Ruda and Escape 135
25. Deportation to the Concentration Camps 139

26. Auschwitz   143
27. Dachau, Camp Number One   147
28. The Sick Camp   152
29. Liberation   157
30. In the Hospital   162
31. The DP Camp   166
32. The Voyage to the United States   171
33. The New Life   173

Maps

Lithuania   2
Kovno City Center   5
Kovno and Its Suburbs   10
The Kovno Ghetto   40

Illustrations follow page 142

Foreword

To say that our understanding of the Holocaust has undergone a drastic change in the half century since the Second World War may at first glance seem obvious. Does not the collective perception of any historical event change with the passage of time, as bits and pieces of information begin to accumulate, as documents and memories gradually sharpen our insight into what happened? Why then should not the picture of the destruction of European Jewry fifty years ago change as well? The process appears entirely natural and normal.

There is more to it than that, however. The way in which we see the Holocaust has become transformed as the murderous act of genocide has gradually ceased to be living actuality and become historical memory. During the first decade or so after the war surprisingly little was written about its most horrifying consequences. It was almost as if the sheer cruelty of mass extermination was more than the outside observer could bear. Only the passage of time made it possible for us to look more closely at the catastrophe that befell the Jewish community. Only the growing distance between us and the victims of the Holocaust enabled us to examine and study their fate.

Yet even after serious study of the destruction of European Jewry began, those who wrote about it generally maintained a certain detachment from the most tragic features of the genocide. They preferred to deal with its technical or administrative aspects, with the way it was planned and executed, with the chain of command and the method of enforcement, with bureaus and bureaucrats, organizations and organizers, with the abstract problems of mass extermination rather than its everyday realities. Thus Gerald Reitlinger's *Final Solution,* published in 1953, and even Raul Hilberg's *Destruction of the European Jews,* which appeared in 1961, tended to obscure or dilute the private agony of the victims of the Holocaust with organizational detail and statistical exactness. They did not ignore the sufferings of millions of ordinary men and women facing destruction, but their emphasis was primarily on the big picture, on the broad effect.

The impersonality of many of these early accounts of the Holocaust derived in part from the sources on which they relied. The victory of the Allies in 1945 meant that historians could examine the captured German documents regarding the planning and execution of the "final solution." They could trace the role of various groups and organizations—the SS, the SD, the Foreign Office, the Wehrmacht and the National Socialist Party—in carrying out the destruction of the Jewish population of Europe. Here was an unparalleled opportunity for scholarly research, and it is no wonder that so many writers rushed to the archives to examine what the architects of genocide had to say about their goals and plans. But this approach to the Holocaust also tended to attenuate or dilute its horror. The tragedy of countless innocent people being rounded up, deported, imprisoned, and executed was mitigated by the bureaucratic language of those who had condemned them to extermination. And this depersonalization of the Holocaust may in fact have been, consciously or unconsciously, a deliberate act.

For a study of the documents left behind by the organizers of the annihilation of European Jewry provides the reader with a measure of protection from the realities of mass murder. They generally deal in technical, dispassionate language with the administrative minutiae of the "final solution." There are official requests for enough transportation to ship so many thousands of men, women, and children from the ghettos to the death camps. There are purchase orders for cement and steel to construct gas chambers and crematories. There are discussions about which poisonous chemicals are capable of killing the largest number of people in the shortest period of time. There are reports from units in the field about the "liquidation" of "communists, partisans, and Jews." There are statistics regarding the number of those condemned to what the documents euphemistically refer to as "night and mist." And all of this is expressed in the dry, impersonal language of bureaucracy, as if describing some business deal or commercial transaction. The official tone of the records helps protect the reader from the stark horror of what they portray.

Only after the Holocaust began to pale in collective memory did it become possible to face its hideousness as an everyday reality. By then the captured German documents had been examined and reexamined, studied and evaluated. There was nothing more to be squeezed out of them. And that was when the focus of study of the destruction of European Jewry started to shift from its perpetrators to its victims. In other words, emphasis on what the Germans had to say gave way to concern with what the Jews had to say. The scrutiny of SS reports and foreign office dispatches was replaced by an interest in the letters, diaries, and memoirs of those who had lived, suffered, and died during the Holocaust. The writings of ghetto dwellers and embattled partisans, of community leaders and despairing intellectuals, of underground fighters and concentration camp prisoners, now became the primary sources for an understanding of the annihilation of the Jewish minority in Europe. The cold bureaucratic report ceased to be the center of scholarly attention. Its place was assumed by the pitiful cries of those who had suffered genocidal agony.

To be sure, some of the survivors of the Holocaust began to publish their memoirs almost as soon as the Second World War was over. But they failed to attract wide attention. For one thing, they were written mostly in languages unfamiliar to readers in Western Europe and America: Yiddish, Hebrew, Polish, or Hungarian. It was easier to study the German documents. More important, these eyewitness accounts described events of such frightfulness that they were almost too painful to contemplate. They aroused feelings of revulsion, distress, shame, or guilt in those who had lived through the period of the Holocaust without being directly affected by it. The victims themselves found it difficult to describe what had happened to them. They preferred to ignore or forget or suppress their recollections. It was still too early to face the past.

Not until the 1960s did the Holocaust recede far enough in public recollection to make possible a direct confrontation with the horrors of genocide. That was when the writings of the men and women who had encountered those horrors began to appear in large numbers, many of them translated into the major European languages. And that in turn meant that a new historical approach to the destruction of European Jewry became possible, based not on the official accounts of those responsible for its execution but on the firsthand experiences of those who had endured its pitilessness. Among the best-known general accounts reflecting this shift of emphasis was Lucy Dawidowicz's *War against the Jews,* which appeared in 1975, and a decade later Martin Gilbert's *Holocaust.* Here the focus was on the thoughts and deeds of countless Jews uprooted from their ancestral homes, segregated in ghettos, hungry, cold, and frightened, condemned to deportation, imprisonment, and mass execution. This was a dimension of the Holocaust which could not be measured by the captured German documents. Only the testimony of those who had faced the reality of genocide was capable of giving true meaning to its inhumanity.

Nevertheless, an important distinction has to be made in the memoir literature between the prominent few who were in a position of authority within the Jewish community and the obscure many who toiled, suffered, hoped, despaired, lived, and died without influence or even comprehension of what was happening around them. To scholars studying the fate of the Jews in Europe during the Second World War, the writings of the former seemed at first far more important. Here were the people who had met and negotiated with the SS, who had to make fateful choices between resistance and collaboration, who had to enforce the will of the occupiers, who had to decide who would live and who would die. They were the ones entrusted with the day-to-day administration of the ghettos in Warsaw and Lodz, Vilna and Kovno, Cracow and Lublin. The responsibility thrust upon them had been enormous.

Foreword xiii

It is thus not surprising that historians of the Holocaust have devoted so much attention to their words and actions. Some of these ghetto leaders used their position to assist fellow Jews, often at great personal risk. Others sought only to save their own skins, obsequiously carrying out the orders of the occupying authorities in the hope of surviving the destruction of their community. But there can be no doubt that they played a major role in the life and death of European Jewry in its last tragic years.

Equally prominent in the memoir literature have been the ghetto chroniclers, those Jews whose education and occupation had trained them to describe from firsthand observation the experiences of a persecuted minority facing annihilation. What they wrote has become a major source of information on the relations between occupiers and occupied, between Christians and Jews, between resisters and collaborators, between the well-to-do, educated Jewish patriciate and the toiling, impoverished Jewish masses. Thanks to them we can still capture the flavor of life for those exposed to rabid anti-Semitism, struggling to survive, hoping for an impossible deliverance, confronting an inescapable destruction. Through their words we can vicariously experience the cruelty of the German occupation, the daily struggle for existence, the unceasing oppression and exploitation, the constant suffering and deprivation, the agonizing march toward death. They provide us with a frightening panorama of a human catastrophe.

Side by side with these chronicles of the destruction of European Jewry, however, a different kind of memoir literature began to emerge, reflecting the experiences not of the elite of education and status within the ghetto but of the meek and the humble. At a time when historical scholarship in general was beginning to view the past from the perspective of ordinary men and women, when it was seeking to construct a new "history from below," the recollections of lowly members of the Jewish community—of workers, farmers, peddlers, and shopkeepers— became increasingly important for an understanding of the Holocaust. These recollections lack the literary style and analytical power of the semiofficial chroniclers. They are by and large unpolished, digressive, and occasionally inaccurate. Yet they give us an insight into the reality of genocide that cannot be obtained from a reading of the memoirs of Jewish leaders and intellectuals. They tell us what life was like for the broad masses of the ghetto population, for those without resources or influence, scrounging for food, begging for shelter, abused, neglected, facing suffering and death. Of all the victims of anti-Semitic fury, they are the most pitiful, the most tragic. Their writings constitute a unique historical literature.

Harry Gordon's memoirs, written in Yiddish in the early 1950s, translated in the early 1970s, are part of that literature. They describe the everyday existence of a Jewish youngster growing up during the period of the German occupation of Lithuania. The style is simple and direct, interspersed with Jewish proverbs and folk sayings, but matter-of-fact, almost casual, free of lamentation or self-pity. The impression it conveys is that this boy enduring the cruelties of a murderous bigotry faced life and death with remarkable steadfastness. Witnessing the extermination of his community and his own family, he displayed a resiliency derived from the conviction that survival was somehow possible, that the barbarity he saw about him would eventually come to an end, and that faith in human goodness must never be completely abandoned. What the source of that conviction was remains unclear. Was it based on some deeply held religious belief? On close family ties and affections? On the sense of cohesiveness within the Jewish community of Kovno in which he lived? Whatever the answer, Mr. Gordon's memoirs reveal extraordinary courage.

The most illuminating sections of the memoirs deal with Jewish life in Lithuania after the German invasion in 1941. Here Mr. Gordon becomes eyewitness to an appalling calamity, to the gradual extermination of a community and a people. Admittedly, there are some aspects of the Holocaust, particularly those concerned with the possible complicity of the victims, on which he remains silent. The young boy, still in his teens, struggling desperately to survive from day to day, had other things on his mind. But Mr. Gordon does provide information on a central problem of the Holocaust. To what degree did

Foreword

non-Germans participate in the persecution and extermination of the Jews? The question is delicate because it touches on the nature of the relationship between the Christian and Jewish communities in Europe before and during the war. In the past the answer usually given has been that the Christians in general sympathized with their Jewish neighbors, that they tried to help them. But what could they do? Those awful Germans let nothing stand in the way of their barbarous plans. That contention, however, has now come to seem superficial or self-serving. It is clear that throughout occupied Europe the German authorities found willing allies in their anti-Semitic campaign. How extensive was this support? What role did it play in the "final solution"? How much did it contribute to the extermination of the Jewish population? On these questions Harry Gordon's memoirs offer significant new evidence. Though dealing only with the situation in Lithuania, they provide, in conjunction with the recollections of survivors of the Holocaust from other parts of Europe, a grim picture of widespread bigotry directed against a helpless, doomed minority.

The ultimate importance of the narrative, however, rests not on what it has to say about this or that unsolved problem of the Holocaust. It lies rather in the unforgettable image of a young boy living in a time of unparalleled cruelty and horror, struggling to survive, displaying remarkable courage, never giving up hope. He saw his closest relatives and friends hounded and imprisoned, innocent people condemned to extermination for being Jews. He himself suffered hardships which seem almost unendurable. And yet he continued to believe, to resist, to fight, and to live. His story is a testimony to the invincibility of the human spirit. It tells us, simply yet vividly, what it was like to experience a terrible historic tragedy, to witness the destruction of an entire people, and to confront and ultimately vanquish the shadow of death.

THEODORE S. HAMEROW
University of Wisconsin-Madison
November 1991

Acknowledgments

Thanks to Mary Ray, who translated my manuscript from the Yiddish so many years ago; to Diane Franzen, who encouraged me to express myself; to Judith Kirkwood, my editor and agent, without whose persistence this book would not have been published; and to Theodore Hamerow, who so generously provided the Foreword.

The maps used in this book are reproduced by permission of the publishers from *Surviving the Holocaust: The Kovno Ghetto Diary* by Avraham Tory, edited by Martin Gilbert (Cambridge, Mass.: Harvard University Press), Copyright © 1990 by the President and Fellows of Harvard College.

1. Before the War

My grandfather's name was Moshe Ganckewitz. I lived with my mother and father in his apartment house at 23 Preplaukos Kanto in Kovno, Lithuania. My grandfather and grandmother (my mother's parents) shared the first floor with us. When I was younger, my mother's two younger sisters, Golda and Celia, lived there too, but after they married they lived with their families in two apartments across from each other on the second floor. An older sister, Ettel, lived with her husband, Abraham Gizelter, a few blocks away until my grandparents died, then they moved in with us on the first floor. Solomon (Shloime), my mother's youngest brother, also lived with us and shared a room with me until he married and moved to the third floor with his wife. The three apartments on the third floor were rented out for approximately ten to fifteen dollars a month (although one tenant paid her rent in eggs). Half the cellar was also rented out to a Kosher butcher shop. The other half was used as an ice house and to store pickles made from my grandfather's cucumbers. We had a Lithuanian janitor who lived three or four miles away and took care of the house and stables for us.

My grandfather was a farmer. He rented land from a Lithuanian landowner to raise his cucumbers. Every Friday morning, around 4:00 or 4:30, he would take the cucumbers to the farmers' market in 150- to 200-pound bags. He had three wagons, each so large that it took two big horses (probably Belgians) to pull it. During school vacations I would ride with the driver the twenty-five or thirty miles to market over rough roads. After the cucumbers were sold we would drive back to the farm and

The Shadow of Death

Grandpa would pull up a chair to a big table and pay off the farmworkers (mostly women) out of a big bag of silver.

Coming home I would get to ride one of the horses down to the river, where we took them to be watered before returning them to the stables. This I loved. When we got home we went through two large doors made of wood and sheet metal that led to the stables in back of the apartment building. There were six stalls and my grandpa kept his carriage there also.

We would have a lunch of soup, rolls, and meat, and then go to the steambath down the street so we would be clean for the *Shabbas*. In the steambath the higher up you went, the hotter it was. I could only make it to the third step, but my Grandpa could go all the way to the tenth step at the top. There was a man called a *pashtek* who would slap you with a beater to stimulate the blood. My grandpa would turn fiery red, but he could have stayed all night. I had to leave after an hour and a half. He would come home after about three hours.

When we came home we would dress to go to the synagogue. The women would be in the kitchen preparing the *Shabbas* meal, but we were never allowed in there for fear someone would give the food the evil eye and jinx it. It smelled delicious, but Aunt Ettel, the oldest sister, was very firm, and no meant no. For *Shabbas* dinner we would have gefilte fish (for which Aunt Ettel was famous), meat, brown potatoes called *cholent,* plums, carrots, soup, and dessert. The whole family—aunts, uncles, and cousins—ate together. I would fall asleep at the table and then be awakened to go to prayers for two hours.

Saturday mornings were also spent at the synagogue unless I could sneak away and play soccer with my friends. But if my mother caught me, she would give me the look and say, "Sit down—don't move," and she meant it. After lunch, usually fresh rolls filled with meat—it would melt in your mouth—we would be so stuffed we would nap for two hours. Then around 3:30 or 4:00 we would all go together for a walk on the main street in Kovna. We lived not far from the president's residence, and we would walk past the stores and shops toward the Capitol and back. Kovno was a beautiful city. About 150,000 people lived there, of whom about 35,000 were Jews. We lived in a mixed neighborhood of Lithuanians and Jews. After two to three hours it was time to go back to the synagogue for a short service. Then we returned home, turned on the lights, had tea and supper, and went to bed.

When I was about seven, my grandfather came home from the steambath one Saturday and had a heart attack. (My grandmother had died when I was quite young; I don't even remember her name.) Since I had been a little boy my grandfather had teased and played with me in the evenings, getting me so excited that my mother would have to tell him over and over to stop. Even so, he would ignore her and continue to play. He had always provided well for his family, giving each of his daughters $10,000 when they married and an apartment in his house so we could all be together. While we were not part of the well-to-do Jewish upper class, we felt prosperous enough and lived comfortably. After grandfather died, Uncle Abraham, the oldest uncle, became head of the family, and what he said was done.

At about that time I started school. It was a Lithuanian school and not many Jews attended, so those who did stuck together. I remember being chased home and beaten up almost every day by one little anti-Semitic bully. I went to school from 8:00 to 3:00 (except on the days I had Hebrew school afterwards) while my mother and aunts stayed home cooking and cleaning and the men went to work. My mother, Eva, worked as a hat designer until she had me. She met my father, Yakob Gordon, in Belgium when she was on her way to the United States. He wanted to travel but came back to Lithuania to live with my mother's family after they fell in love and married. I was born on July 5, 1925. I remember my mother looking out our windows at the women walking by on the streets and sketching their hats. My father started out in the fur business, like his brother Leib, but after a few months became a mechanic in a textile factory.

Uncle Abraham, Ettel's husband, was a tailor. Before he married, he would go to the United States for the tailoring season and stay three to four months. He made good money but was always glad to come back to Kovno. He thought the Americans lived too fast and too crazy. Uncle Borach Shapiro, Celia's husband, was a traveling salesman who sold china and candy

Before the War

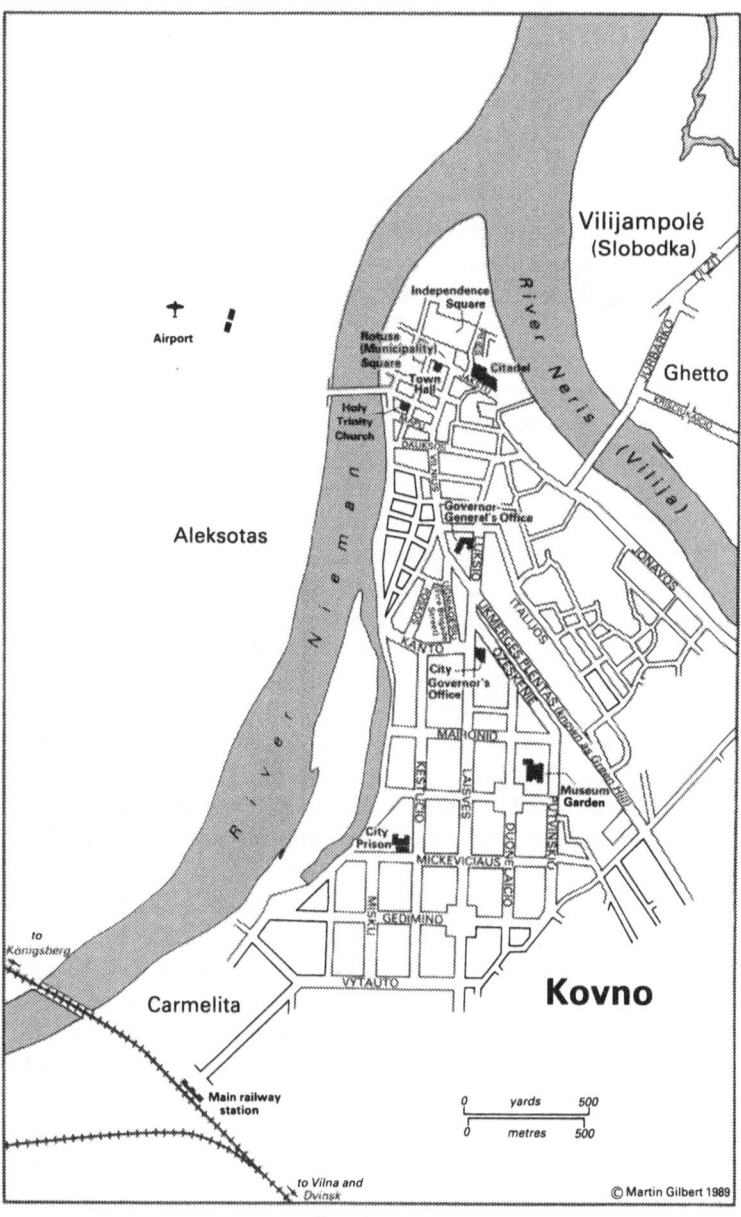

Kovno city center

and other things. I used to love it when he brought samples home. He had a car and a chauffeur. Uncle Yenchik Panemunsky, Golda's husband, was a big, strong man who bought cattle to sell to slaughterhouses. To determine the weight of the animals, he would lift them!

My mother's three older brothers—Jack, Beryl, and Alex they were called in America—had gone to New York City in the 1920s. When their businesses went under during the Depression, Alex and Beryl moved to Buffalo, where Alex managed four to five clothing stores and Beryl owned and ran two filling stations and a tavern. Jack moved to Bear Lake, Pennsylvania (near Erie), where he had a mink farm. They had changed their name from Ganckewitz to Ginsberg, but this we didn't know at the time. They used to send us packages of clothes. I was the best dressed boy in the school. I remember particularly a navy blue sailor suit that I had my picture taken in.

Every night there were twenty-five to thirty people at our house, either for supper or visiting afterward. The men came home from work at about five o'clock, and everyone came to our apartment. At supper the men talked about work and what had happened during the day. After, while the women washed dishes and gossiped in the kitchen, the men played cards and gambled, telling stories about their lives. I would usually stand behind Uncle Abraham, looking at the cards over his shoulder and listening to these tales. Around 7:00 or 8:00 more people would stop by and I would hear their voices buzzing as I dropped off to sleep in the bedroom.

One time I heard a story about Uncle Yenchik Panemunsky. In the winter the river Nemonas (Nieman) was frozen and Uncle Yenchik, who lived on the other side, in Marivanka, would come across on the ice. He was known to carry a lot of money and one night four men tried to rob him. But he had a terrible temper, and when he was through with them, two were almost dead and the other two ran for their lives. Another time I heard the women in the kitchen whispering about hiring a matchmaker for Aunt Golda, who at twenty-five had still not married. And that was how she and Uncle Yenchik got together.

I also remember the night Aunt Celia called the family together and, with Borach Shapiro, announced their plans to marry in a month. The whole family went crazy kissing and hugging, hollering *"Mazel tov!"* Immediately the women began talking about what had to be done. Soon they were baking *teyglach*, pastries. They rented a big hall and had an orchestra, and wine and booze were plentiful. All the *mechatonim*, the new in-laws, ran around having a good time. For months after, everyone talked about it. Aunt Celia and Uncle Borach moved in on the second floor and bought brand new furniture. Everything was arranged nicely and the floors were so clean you could eat off them.

Around that time, my mother's youngest brother, Shloime, for some reason we didn't understand, had to register with the Lithuanian army and was called up for service. There was much discussion of what we should do—arrange for him to go to the United States to his brothers? Pay off the authorities to dismiss him? But in the end he had to go. He would come home for one or two days a month on furlough, and the aunts would complain about how thin he looked, as if he had TB. We thought he had lost about fifty pounds. "Don't make such a big fuss," he would say. "It's not so bad. I get enough food." But, of course, he had to eat *chazer*, pig, in the army. The family was afraid he would turn into a *goy*. Once when he was home he was sitting on the bed in the room we shared and eating some meat that looked good to me. It looked like Kosher corned beef. I asked him if I could have some, and it tasted good. I was enjoying it when my mother came in the room and saw me eating this ham. *"Oy veh!"* She started running around and hollering that I was a *chazer*, that I had a *dybbuk*, a devil, in me from eating that meat.

In the summers my mother and I would go to my Aunt Ettel and Uncle Abraham's resort in a small town not far away. We took a boat down the river to get there. From May to September they operated a small restaurant and motel, and my mother would help with the cooking. My father and others would come out on the weekends. Twenty-five or thirty vacationers would stay there, but at dinnertime the restaurant was packed. I talked my uncle into buying a ping-pong table and used to win money playing table tennis with the tourists. By the end of the summer I would have about twenty-five to fifty dollars in my pocket, which was quite a lot for a boy my age at that time.

I was spoiled by Uncle Abraham and Aunt Ettel. They had no children of their own so I was like a son to them. They bought me many things, including a beautiful gold watch. But the best thing was a brand new bike. Actually, my uncle had won about $50,000 in the lottery one summer and used some of that to buy me the bicycle. I kept it in my room so it wouldn't get dusty. Where I went, it went with me. I was so proud of it. I was overwhelmed with joy I could hardly express.

When I was about twelve and a half my parents hired a rabbi to come to the house to tutor me for my Bar Mitzvah. I studied so hard I could say the prayers in my sleep. When the big day came I was nervous, but as I looked at my family sitting out there—my mother and father, my uncles, aunts, and cousins—I was able to recite my prayers beautifully. Afterward we must have had two hundred people in our living room for a party. I got so many presents I could have opened a store. But the best thing was that now I was a *mensch,* a grown man. I was full of hopes and dreams for the future.

But, as the saying goes, "Just as you begin to live, you die."

2. The Russian Invasion

One Saturday afternoon—it was in June 1940—we were going for a walk as usual down the main street of Kovno when suddenly we heard loud noises. From all sides there appeared military tanks. They came across the two bridges over the rivers, moving fast. They were closed so we couldn't see anyone. We thought the Germans were coming. We didn't know what was happening.

We knew, from the newspapers and the radio, that the Germans were trying to take over all of Europe. They had taken Poland, France, everybody, so we thought these were Germans. Right away panic started. People were running into their homes to hide, especially the Jewish population, because we had heard, we knew, what they were doing in the other countries—they were coming in and sending Jews to ghettos, to concentration camps. We thought that if they were coming, that was what they were going to do with us, too. After all, we Lithuanian Jews were no better than any other Jewish population. But as the tanks slowed down and we looked more carefully out our windows, we saw the red stars and knew these were not the Germans but the Russians.

Suddenly our mood changed. Instead of panic, we felt an unnatural joy. Everyone started hugging and kissing each other, family and neighbors, as if the Messiah had just arrived. Although we didn't know it yet, we were lying between two hungry animals, but the Germans were the worse of the two. Those who had been hiding ran out of their houses and began throwing

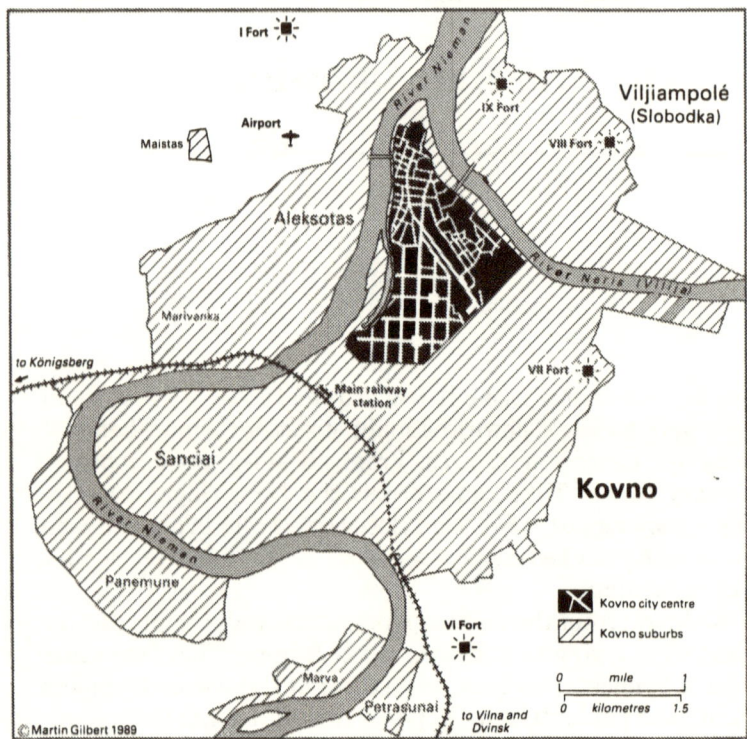

Kovno and its suburbs

bouquets of flowers at the approaching army. At any moment, the Germans could have swallowed us up, but here, suddenly, there was a miracle. The Red Army was marching into Lithuania.

From the tanks the Red Army soldiers were throwing out Russian cigarettes, chocolate and other candy. When they passed little children in buggies, they jumped off the tanks and ran up to ask the parents for their names and address so they could take the children for rides on the tanks, bringing them back in the evening. The streets were filled with people, young and old, running to see the Red Army. Then the real thing began: the foot soldiers came marching in, and buggies, each pulled by four horses and with two soldiers and a machine gun on top. Always one of the soldiers played a harmonica while the second drove the horses and sang. No army in the world could play and sing and dance like the Russian army. The singing was so beautiful that many people of the town stayed outside day and night to watch and listen, sleeping in the street with little children who didn't think about eating, drinking, or sleeping.

I stayed in the streets, too. My mother tried to persuade me to come home. "Let's go home and eat," she would say as she pulled on my arm. "You can't stay here all the time and not eat anything. You will have enough times to go hungry." I would tear away from her to run to a different place where she couldn't find me. She didn't want to run after me so she went home and made me some sandwiches and brought them to me to eat in the street. Since I was hungry I became better behaved and more appreciative. Still, as I stuffed my sandwich in my mouth, I had ears and eyes only for the Red Army, to hear their music and see them dance. Running back and forth, I must have looked like Charlie Chaplin working on the assembly line in a scene from *Modern Times*.

The Lithuanian police from the old democratic republic, dressed in their blue coats with gold buttons and their round caps with white plumes, were still at their posts as the Russian army poured in. They were very demoralized. They knew their country was being taken over, yet they still had to try to keep order. It took a week of marching day and night for the army to move through the town. During this time the young Communists, some of them Jewish, had quite a celebration. They insulted the Lithuanian police, laughed about the president, Antanas Smetona, who had run to Germany, and told exaggerated stories about the Lithuanian police beating up Jews. This antagonized the whole Lithuanian population.

Eventually conditions became more normal as the government became more organized. The Lithuanian Communists put in their own president, Justas Paleckis, and put their own people in state and local government jobs. Lithuania was annexed to Russia and renamed the Lithuanian Russian Republic. Later the Lithuanian government leaders would be shown to have sold out to the Germans.

At this time, they began hiring Jews at the NKVD, the Russian FBI, and many Jews became food distributors to the Russian army. They appeared to become very rich from this, but the wealth meant nothing because Russian rubles were worthless. It was ridiculous to equate a ten-dollar Lithuanian bill with Russian money because Lithuanian money was backed by gold and Russian money was backed by nothing.

The Lithuanian Communists issued an order that all cabarets, cafés, taverns, shops, and stores had to be open twenty-four hours a day to accommodate the soldiers. Lithuania was a prosperous country with all kinds of merchandise. To these Russian soldiers it was like being in heaven. They had never seen so many things and so much food. They had brought with them bags of rubles which they had saved, since there was nothing to buy in Russia, and would buy anything that came into their hands; they would never say that they didn't want something. The main thing they wanted was wristwatches, for they were wearing big alarm clocks strapped to their wrists, which must have torn up their arms. You could stand a mile away from them and hear the ticking of the clocks as if each had inside nothing but a large hammer.

They began running to the stores to buy up everything, and this started a panic for the merchants; every day the soldiers bought out several stores, and the merchants were left with no goods and no way to replace their stock. The smarter merchants, who could see what was ahead, began to hide their better merchandise when they saw the Red Army coming like a horde of locusts. They left out all the junk they hadn't been able to get rid of before the army came. They had to leave something in their stores, for if the government found out they were refusing to sell anything they would be taken to jail or fined heavily. After the store was empty, a government comptroller would come in to search for hidden merchandise. If he found anything, the merchant and his family disappeared and were never heard of again.

One day I was in a shoe store when some soldiers came in. To their despair the merchant didn't have anything in their size; he only had about five pairs of shoes in sizes eight and nine left.

The soldiers went out, feeling sorry for themselves, and ran to the next store, hoping for better luck. All of a sudden the door opened again and in ran a soldier looking half dead and half alive. He was sweaty and couldn't say a word because he was out of breath. The merchant asked him what he wanted.

"I have already been all over town," he said, "in all the stores. I can't find any shoes in my size."

"What size do you wear?"

"Size seven."

"I'm sorry," the merchant replied, "I only have sizes bigger than you can use."

"Please, let me try them on. Maybe they will fit."

The merchant brought in a pair of shoes and the soldier tried them on. He started walking around and it was obvious that he was swimming in them. But he asked, "How many pairs of shoes like this do you have?"

"I have only five pairs of shoes left in all the store."

"Box up all five pairs, then," the soldier said.

The salesman thought he was joking at first, but he looked very sincere and was taking rubles from his bag and counting how many he would need to buy five pairs. Seeing that he was serious, the merchant said, "That's all the shoes I have! You can't take all my stock. They don't even fit you. Your friends, the other soldiers, need shoes too."

The soldier wouldn't hear any of it. He said he would pay for them, whatever the cost. "Pack them up. I'll be back in half an hour."

Thirty minutes later he came back with a truck and picked up all the shoes. This happened in all the stores—with jewelry, dresses, furniture, even groceries.

Why did he buy five pairs of shoes that didn't even fit him? The answer is simple. Every soldier had relatives in Russia—parents, brothers, cousins—so that however much he bought there was never enough. Whatever he couldn't use he could send back to his family. Thus the buying lasted until there was nothing left to buy.

How did the merchants make a living once their stock was gone? They went to work for the Russians. In fact, this contributed to the anti-Semitism of the Lithuanians because they saw the Russians hiring many Jews for jobs they would have liked to have. The Russians seemed to prefer the Jewish workers—maybe they were easier to get along with, since the Lithuanians were pro-German and couldn't wait to see the Russians driven out.

When there was nothing left to buy, the soldiers started working on the restaurants, theaters, and cabarets, buying vodka and liquor. But they were ordered not to drink too much and to be very polite in order to set a good example for the Lithuanian army.

They began to look for places to live in the town so they could bring in their wives and children from Russia. Once I was near the train station when some Russian officers were picking up their wives. The express arrived and the women began to get off, some from Moscow and some from deep Russia. I saw a woman coming off the platform with her husband, who was a flier, taking her by the arm. She was dressed so poorly that her appearance almost made me sick! She wore a big red beret, a dark jacket with many holes in it, a pair of men's socks and men's shoes, and on her hands a pair of white gloves. All the rest of the women arriving looked the same except that some wore different colors and some carried babies in their arms, wrapped in shawls.

In only a few weeks, though, you wouldn't recognize these women in the furs and beautiful jackets their husbands bought for them. But they thought the beautiful nightgowns embroidered with monograms and flowers that their husbands bought for them were lovely evening gowns. They wore them to the ballet and to the theater before they learned their mistake. Eventually they learned to be as stylish as so many French women.

A Russian officer, a pilot, rented a room in our house, which was close to the airfield. He rented a room in Aunt Golda's apartment on the second floor. Since we wanted to find out what was going on in Russia, how the Jewish people lived and what the overall situation was there, my family decided to invite the flier to come to dinner so we could talk. He came and we sat down to eat. We asked him if he would like to have a drink, but he refused; he said that he did not drink at all. "A Russian who doesn't drink?" we wondered. We couldn't believe it. A Russian, for vodka, would sell his mother, his father, even his leader, Stalin! Still, he said that he didn't drink but he *did* eat. We got a little scared; we didn't want to pry. If we asked him questions, all he had to do was go to the NKVD and report us, and that would be the end of our lives. All in all, we couldn't get anything out of him. We invited him a second night and a third, but he wouldn't drink so we couldn't get him to talk. We thought for sure we had found the first Russian who didn't drink.

One nice evening, as my uncles were coming in from the street, they saw the officer in the hallway drinking something. It was dark in the hall and they couldn't see what he was drinking so they thought it was sodapop.

"How come you are standing here in the hall where it's dark? You can come into the house. The doors are open," they said.

He didn't answer and they became a little suspicious. They had become fairly friendly with him, and now he wouldn't even speak to them. When he started to walk he was staggering, so they took him by each arm and led him into the house, where they saw that he was holding not vodka or some other liquor but something a lot worse: half a bottle of fuel used in gas lamps!

Even with that alcohol, his mind was still in very good shape. We started asking him questions, but we couldn't get anything out of him. My uncles took him up to his room and put him to bed and he fell asleep immediately.

The next morning when he got up he remembered what had happened the night before and felt very embarrassed. He came down to see us and apologized. Right then he started talking. The ice was broken. He told us why he didn't want to drink in our house; he had an order from the commandant not to drink in front of the civilian population. If he were caught breaking that order he would be sent to Siberia. The officers had also been told to be very polite to the civilians.

The manners of the Russian soldiers were excellent. They weren't like the Cossacks, riding through town and terrorizing innocent civilians. These soldiers were learned and informed.

Every soldier carried a map and knew exactly in what part of the country he was, how to act with the people, and how to express himself with them. Russia was a very young country with many different cultures and it was unbelievable to us that the soldiers had such a high level of understanding of another country.

The Jewish people felt very free. This was not too bad. No impoliteness was allowed; this was true for the Russians, Jews, and Lithuanians. No one could call us names or insult us because if they did they would be sent to jail for six months. Every Jew held his head high. If he met a Lithuanian on the sidewalk, the Lithuanian would step off the curb to let him by. Before the Russians came, it had been just the reverse. The anti-Semites' eyes were popping out of their heads from the pressure of having to keep their mouths shut! But there were some who just couldn't hold their tongues. Even with the threat of never seeing the light of day again they still would take the risk and speak: "Hey, you! Jew! You think that Stalin is your Daddy? You think you are in heaven? It isn't going to last! Even with this treaty between Hitler and Stalin, there still will be war between Germany and Russia and then we will show you what we can do!" If someone informed the NKVD, the man would not be seen again. But even with that they continued to taunt us.

There is a Jewish saying: "If we are on the horse today, then the Lithuanians are ten feet under." We would enjoy it while it lasted. What would happen later we didn't want to know. We lived for the day. But the anti-Semites knew what they were talking about; what they would show us we would remember for generations to come.

Life went on. When we went down the street for a walk, we would see on every block groups of ten or twelve people in the middle of which would be three Red Army soldiers, one playing a harmonica, one singing, and one dancing the traditional Cossack dances. The Lithuanian police would be around also, to keep order.

After the Russian officers had brought in their families and had nice homes and clothing, they began compiling lists on the population of Kovno to find out what kind of affiliations the Lithuanians and Lithuanian Jews had. They wanted information as to nationalities and political parties, and they went through all the records to find this information on each citizen. At the same time they began to encourage the young people to join the Communist organizations. School children were required to join the Communist party and to participate in the Communist lectures. Anyone who refused to attend was considered an enemy of the state; he and his family were kept under close surveillance. I went to their indoctrination classes as a student, but I really don't remember much about them.

If it was discovered that you were a Democrat or a Zionist, or just that you didn't like the Russians, soldiers would come in the middle of the night and take you away. Where people were taken, no one knew. But as more people found out that this was happening, some disappeared from the city and hid out.

The Lithuanians were getting pulled into more Communist activities daily. After dissolving the Lithuanian forces the Russian army began taking Lithuanian recruits and training them, taking them into deep Russia. From deep Russia they transported Russian recruits to Lithuania, very young men.

The Russian soldiers came to the steambath near our house. After a bath, they would teach the young recruits how to march, singing while they did so. I didn't like the marching, but the singing made me feel very mellow.

The soldiers also tried to indoctrinate the Lithuanian children. Once I saw a little boy, maybe four years old, walking, holding his mother's hand. A Russian soldier ran up and took him in his arms and asked the child if he would like a piece of candy. What child would say no? When the boy said yes, the soldier told him to close his eyes and ask God, "Hey God, give me some candy," three times. The boy did this and the soldier told him to look in his hand to see if he had gotten any candy.

The child said, "No, God is bad. He didn't give me any candy."

The soldier then told him, "Close your eyes and ask me for candy three times." The little boy did this, and after the first time the soldier put a piece of candy in his mouth. When he felt the candy, the child opened his eyes and a big smile appeared on his face.

The soldier asked him, "Who gave you the candy, God or me?"

"You!"

"Then who do you love more, God or me?"

"You," answered the child. In this way they were starting from the beginning to take religious feelings from children and implant the Communist way of thinking. I am sure that Red Army soldier had had the same experience when he was a child. This training was the foundation on which they built the Communist regime. They based it on the very young because they knew they would not be able to take the faith away from the older people.

In time, an order nationalizing all factories, apartment houses, and any house larger than 120 square meters (about 1,300 square feet) was issued. Our house was nationalized, too. Suddenly, it was no longer ours. But we still lived there, so we didn't think too much about it at the time.

The owners of the factories were removed and in their place the Russians appointed their own managers, or commissars, to run things. Sometimes they chose the man working in the factory with the most seniority (even if he happened to be a janitor), sometimes a Communist party member who worked in the factory.

Can you imagine what a good time this was for those who now became bosses? If a person thought the old boss had been unfair, he could now enjoy giving him a hard time, especially if that boss had been brought back to work under him in the factory. I would see the new commissars walking down the street in their shiny leather boots, their potbellies hanging out, blowing cigarette smoke and feeling sure that the whole world was watching them. They were certain that, in the Kremlin, they were discussing the work of these Lithuanian commissars.

The Russians tried to get the workers to think, "Look what Stalin has done for me; just a little while ago I was a janitor and now I run a large factory!" In fact, my father got a promotion at his factory at that time. But in truth, that same working man who became the commissar had been able to live better on his wages as a worker before the Communist takeover than he could as a commissar. The smarter ones came to realize this, but the stupid ones didn't. It was also true that not every worker could become a commissar, since there weren't a great many factories in Lithuania, which was mostly an agricultural country.

The factories began to have problems; the owners had known where to buy and sell and had had a network of business friends. Now this knowledge was lost. Former owners did not want to return to the factories after the state took over. Production began to decline and each factory was like a boat without a captain. At first the workers did not realize it, but wages began to drop and food became more scarce in the city as Russians shipped carloads of grain, dairy products, and other foods into Russia.

In Russia, a worker couldn't make a living at his normal job; he couldn't support his family. In order to survive, he had to steal, and the Russian government knew this. In all the factories and offices there was theft by workers and officials, even though being caught meant becoming a commissar in Siberia. The government encouraged the development of fastworkers to help alleviate this, for a fastworker could earn a living with his bonuses so that he would not have to steal, the government didn't care about the quality of his work. If he produced 500 yards of cloth, they didn't care if 100 of those yards had to be discarded as unusable later; they simply raised the price of the material to cover the cost of the loss. Therefore, in Russia, one had to be a high government official to be able to afford enough material for a new suit.

The Russians began to build this same kind of system in Lithuania, although things were still not as high as in Russia. We heard that in Russia a working man got 350 rubles a month, which was the same wage as in Lithuania; but in Russia two pounds of butter cost 650 rubbles, and butter was not available at all except in Moscow. Everything produced on the large Russian farms was sent to Moscow to be apportioned to the various districts of the country and was sold in large cooperatives there. The Lithuanian workers gradually got ideas from the Russians as to how things were in Russia, and they weren't impressed. Unlike the Russians, the Lithuanians had known a better life and thus knew what they were missing. They began to realize that not all could become fastworkers or commissars; they began to awaken from their sleep. But it was too late. The Russians were already in control.

They began shipping machinery to Russia from the Lithuanian factories. Soon they were dismantling and sending whole factories, and the people who had worked in them were left without work. The workers became afraid they were going to be shipped to Russia with the factories. How would they make a living?

In March 1941 an order was issued that all German citizens in newly annexed Russian territory had to return to Germany; German soldiers would come to pick them up. This was very upsetting to us, for we Jews now realized that war between Germany and Russia was imminent. It was only a question of time. Even the Russians themselves knew that and talked about it.

German trucks appeared to chauffeur the German citizens out of Lithuania. Immediately after the Germans finished their evacuation the Russians began fortifying the border quietly, moving most of their equipment and troops at night. They also began deporting Jews and Lithuanians into deep Russia.

We began to feel more panic, even though the Russians tried to avoid this by doing their work at night. The Russian government requested a new census from the Lithuanian Communist government, listing how many Lithuanians there were and what political parties they belonged to. They especially wanted to know the loyalties of the young Lithuanians. The new government betrayed them, however; they purposely gave them false surveys, listing the old and sick and the Jews but omitting the young Lithuanians, who planned to become guerrillas to aid the Germans. The Lithuanian Communist government did advocate communism, but it was both anti-Semitic and anti-Russian.

The Russians began deporting large groups of people to Siberia. They wanted to take possible subversives away from the border, but instead they got the old and ill and the Jewish people on the list. Each night they drove up in large wood-burning trucks to the homes of families and knocked on their doors. People would run to the door and open it, half-dead with fear, as two soldiers rushed in with carbines aimed, telling them to dress quickly and get in the truck. They allowed no time for packing even extra clothes but took people quickly to the trains. At the depot boxcars were waiting, and the people were loaded onto them like animals, one hundred and fifty to two hundred in a car. Each car had only one small window for ventilation, which was covered with barbed wire to prevent escapes. On each boxcar, written in Russian in large white letters, were the words "traitor to the country."

Every day we heard about this person or that family being taken. Everyone walked around as if in a daze, not knowing what to do, each counting the days until his turn would come. We could not sleep at night. Any noise from the trucks would send us running to the door. We would get dressed and then see that the truck had stopped at a neighbor's up the street.

Can you understand how we felt, seeing our neighbors taken? We were in shock; any noise we heard sounded like a knock at the door. We were completely demoralized and lived like this day after day, without knowing when, why, or what. Like the Romans defending their gods, anyone who didn't follow the Communist line and Stalin's constitution was fed to the lions. Our world was crumbling, and the life we had lived until then was already dead.

3. The War Begins

During the last year, when we were living under Russian Communist rule, some things remained the same. My father was still at the textile factory and had even gotten a promotion. Uncle Borach worked as a commissar, supplying the Russian army with food. And Uncle Yenchik was still in the cattle business. I went to school every day and we went to *shul* on Friday and Saturday. The rabbis never mentioned the political situation; they spent their time talking about miracles. We still ate and talked together in the evenings. We really hadn't experienced any food shortages, and our financial situation was stable.

But when the Germans left and people began being deported to Russia, we knew things were more serious and our days were numbered. I had begun to think about leaving Lithuania, but no one else in the family talked about it. I don't know if it would have been possible even if we had had the money to get out. When we saw our neighbors' families being torn apart, we didn't know what to do.

We were even more worried because my mother had hepatitis or appendicitis and was so sick we had to take her to the hospital for four to five weeks. She came home for a few days, but her pain was so great that she had to return. Every day after school I went to visit her at the Jewish hospital. She loved me very much, especially since I was her only child. I was more understanding and attentive than most children my age and she also loved me for that.

After my mother returned to the hospital, the Russians started deporting people at a faster pace. What would happen to

The War Begins

my mother if they came back and took our family to Russia? We could not take her with us for she was too sick, but if we were taken and she were left behind, it would tear her to pieces. We were not committed to any party, Democratic or Communist or Zionist—in fact we had nothing to do with politics—but we had heard that they were now taking nonparty members.

Uncle Abraham decided, and we agreed, that if the Russians came to take us to Siberia, we would leave the house, furniture, and all our belongings to the Lithuanian janitor who helped take care of the house and stables. We had known this man and his daughter for a long time. His daughter, Raisa, was in her thirties. She could speak Yiddish better than I could, and Russian too. At this time there was a saying, "A Lithuanian who speaks Yiddish and a chicken who squawks, you have to chop off their heads." We thought if we were lucky enough to live through the war, we would come back and our janitor would return our possessions. Man was thinking, but God was laughing. The Russians didn't take us to Siberia; they didn't have time.

June 22, 1941, the first day of the war, was a Sunday morning. The sun was just peering through the shadows of the houses and the grass was covered with dew. The birds sang so sadly that it seemed they also felt that a black cloud was coming over us. At five o'clock in the morning I heard such a heavy pounding that the whole house shook and my bed moved back and forth as if it were an earthquake. I jumped out of bed and ran to my father to ask him what it was. My father had also been awakened; he told me that it was the Russians on aviation maneuvers and that I should go back to bed.

I had just fallen asleep when the house started to shake again. It was impossible to lie in bed, much less sleep. I ran to the window and opened the shutters. Across the lake on a high hill I saw a big black cloud of smoke. What this meant I didn't know. I called to my father to look. We dressed and went out into the street. Already people were standing in groups talking to each other in whispers. Those who had been listening to their radios that morning had heard that Germany had declared war against Russia. This declaration was transmitted at 6:00 AM, but the

Russian airfields had been bombarded at 4:00 AM—not just one, but all the Lithuanian bases. Lithuania, Estonia, Latvia, and Minsk had all been attacked. The cloud we had seen came from nearby Aleksotas airfield.

The Russians themselves didn't know what had happened; most were drunk from Saturday night and many were asleep in the cabarets. The Russian who lived with us had not gone out the night before, so as soon as he heard the commotion he rushed to the Russian commander, who told him the Germans had declared war and that he should report to his plane and receive orders there. He came back and told us it was war and that he had to report right away. In less than half and hour, however, he was back; but he was not the same. His complexion was mottled and he didn't know what to say. All the planes were destroyed, burned. Nobody was there. He went to his room and got his suitcase. Saying goodby quickly, he ran away. He must have known what was happening.

The whole Russian leadership had already deserted to the Germans. Many Russian soldiers were running back toward Russia. All the Russian army in Lithuania had no mother or father; everyone could do as he wanted. At one o'clock in the afternoon you could already see Russian soldiers fleeing the front line, one without a rifle, another without a boot. They stopped at houses to ask for food. Suddenly we could see the German airplanes trying to bombard the running army. The Germans knew they were demoralized and were flying low and shooting the Russians down with machine guns. The soldiers ran into the houses and, hiding in the halls, began shooting at the planes with their rifles, doing no good.

It was the first day of war, yet it looked like it had been going on for a year. As they saw the chaos in the Russian army, the young Lithuanians started sniping at the running soldiers, shooting them in the back. The Russians didn't know what was going on or what kind of country they were in; they ran one way and another. We saw twelve Russians on horses galloping toward the trains; at the same time we saw a machine gun appear at the second floor window of a nearby house, and suddenly the twelve men were dead. Russian families with women and children were rushing in loaded trucks to the trains. Everyone was running without knowing where they were going.

We decided to run with the Russians, for it was better than being killed by the Germans or Lithuanians. Each of us took a small suitcase filled with food, and together we started down the road. All the roads and bridges were jammed with the Russian army. The German bombers were flying overhead. With us were many other Jewish families who didn't want to fall into the hands of the German beast. We thought we could reach the Russian border before the Germans could capture us, but the Germans were coming too fast.

After several days the German paratroopers landed by the hundreds to cut off the deserting Russian army. The fighting began and we were in the middle. Bullets were flying over our heads and people were falling dead like flies. Heads, hands, and legs were torn off. There was only sky and dirt. To our despair, we realized that we had made a mistake. We wouldn't have enough strength to reach the Russian border and the Germans wouldn't let us, anyway. We had been on the road a week and decided to stay right where we were, about 200 miles from Kovno, and see what happened. We thought perhaps the Russians would be able to stop the German offensive and then we would go farther. If the Russians didn't stop them we would try to go back home.

The German attack intensified. We heard that the Germans were already in Vilna, so it made no sense to run because we had to go through Vilna. We started back toward home, traveling at night and sleeping in the woods during the day. We had to make our way through several different battles between the Germans and the Russians, some of which were pretty rugged. The Russians fought bitterly for every square meter of land, but they had no leadership.

We met other Jewish families trying to flee from the Germans, some of whom had made it to the Russian border only to be turned back. Not only would the Russians not let them in, they would not even let Russian Communists cross the border; they told them to stay behind the lines and see if they could help the party there. We also learned from these Jewish refugees that all the people taken in boxcars to Russia, both the Jewish and Lithuanian prisoners and the Russian evacuees, had been killed by German bombs. As we walked toward home we began to see more and more German personnel and very few Russians. On the roads around us were dead horses and dead people—women and children, but mostly Russian soldiers.

The fiercest of the Russian soldiers were the Kalmiuks, who were Mongolians and would fight until their last breath. They did not want to be taken alive as prisoners, and the Germans were afraid to take them, preferring to shoot them on the spot. I saw two German soldiers holding a Kalmiuk prisoner at gunpoint. Suddenly the Kalmiuk jumped toward one soldier and caught his adam's apple in his teeth, ripping it from his throat. The German fell dead and the second soldier began shooting at the Kalmiuk with his rifle, one bullet after another. I could count the bullets going into that Russian, who carried a knife with his teeth as he crawled toward the German to kill him. He was too weak to succeed, and he died with the knife still between his teeth.

As we neared Kovno, we heard that the Germans were there and that the Lithuanians were already having fun with Jewish blood. As we walked down the road we saw a high German officer coming toward us on a motorcycle, well-fed, looking like a pig and also looking a little drunk. He stopped his motorcycle beside us and asked us who we were and where we were coming from. We told him that we were Jews.

"Oh, Jews, huh? You must be Communists and you wanted to run with the Russians, but you couldn't do it, could you?" he said with an ironic smile. "I suppose now you are going back home. Now we are going to show you, you Jews, Communists!"

A family traveling with us had a beautiful daughter; the German asked her how old she was and she answered she was eighteen. He looked at all of us, then spoke to the girl, "Come with me." Can you understand how we all felt? We began to tremble. The girl understood what he had in mind, and she pretended that she didn't hear what he said. He pulled out his gun and said, "If you don't come with me right now I will kill you right here and kill not just you, but everyone else with you." The girl had no alternative, so she went with him.

The War Begins

He took her down the road and in fifteen or twenty minutes came back, got on his motorcycle and told all of us that we could go as he drove off. The parents walked down the road where he had taken the girl. There by the side of the road they saw an awful picture; the girl laying, raped, in a pool of blood where he had shot her. This was the beginning of real misery. The parents stood looking at the sight, at what had happened to their only child, and they didn't want to move from the spot. My family tried to get them to come with us and continue the journey home, but they would not move. We could do nothing. I have no idea what happened to that family.

As we approached Kovno, around 5:00 PM, our worst fears were not of the Germans but of the Lithuanians. When we reached the edge of the city our family divided into small groups so that we would be less noticeable. We agreed to go each a different way and meet at our house.

As I walked with my father, Aunt Ettel, and Uncle Abraham, we saw German and Lithuanian signs hanging from formerly Jewish stores. The doors of many Jewish homes were sealed. The Lithuanians knew that when the Russians pulled out the Jews would flee with them, so they had gone through the Jewish neighborhoods sealing the homes. In that way they would know if the Jews came back and tried to break the seals. The Lithuanians would then seize them for breaking and entering. This happened with many Jews; they came back, broke the seals, and the next morning were found murdered in their own homes.

There was no seal on our house because the Lithuanian janitor and his daughter had already moved in, assuming that we were dead. They were anxious to inherit the house and our possessions. Seeing us come back, they looked as if they were seeing ghosts. They put on a big act of being glad to see us, crying out of their third eye, saying that they had not known what was happening to us. They told us that we should hide immediately because each day the Lithuanian partisans came to the house to ask if there were any Jews, planning to kill them. We went up into the attic and lay there on the floor, trembling at any sound or movement in the yard. We were very afraid that our great Lithuanian friend and his daughter would turn us in to the partisans, and this is what they did—but not right away.

We were concerned about my mother in the hospital. We didn't know what was happening there or how she was, so we decided that I would go the next morning to the hospital and find out if we could bring her home. This was a very dangerous proposition, and I was playing with my life, but since I spoke Lithuanian well, and since I looked more Lithuanian than Jewish (at least that is what people had always told me), and also since, being short, I looked like a young boy, even though I was sixteen, I was the one to take a chance.

All night, lying there, thinking about the next day, I wondered what I would say when I saw my mother; all sorts of things ran through my mind. As soon as morning arrived, I crawled down from the attic and started toward the hospital by way of the alleys and fencerows so that no one would notice me. As I walked through each yard, I saw tragedy. Dead bodies everywhere. The gutters were filled with Jewish blood. I wanted to turn around and go home, but I was almost halfway to the hospital. I thought I would see my mother soon, and that gave me courage.

When I saw the steps of the hospital all my fear turned to happiness because soon I would be with my mother, talk to her, and tell her not to be afraid, that we were all alive and all together and we would take her home. At the information window a Lithuanian girl looked out and asked me in Lithuanian what I wanted. She was sitting where before there had been a Jewish man. I told her that I wished to see my sick mother. She asked for my name and told me to wait, closing the window. As I waited I got more nervous. Finally, the window opened halfway and the girl said, "I'm sorry. Your mother is dead."

I don't know what happened to me at that moment, but when I roused as from a sleep I was sitting on a bench in the hospital. I felt so hopeless. The Lithuanian girl gave me some water and told me that if I wanted to I could go see my mother's body in the hospital morgue. Since she had just died the day before I might be able to recognize her.

I went down to the morgue and a Lithuanian doctor asked me what I was looking for. I told him, "I want to see my dead mother one more time."

The War Begins

In Lithuanian he told me, "There are five hundred dead bodies here, all dead from poisoning, which turned the bodies dark. You want to find your mother? All the corpses look alike; how can you identify your mother?"

I didn't ask any more questions. Slowly I pushed myself out of the morgue. Before my eyes I saw many different colors like stars and I felt as if my feet had been knocked out from under me. My head was pounding with the feeling that my mother was still alive and was talking to me.

"Hershke, my only son. Why didn't you come to me a day earlier? You know how much I loved you. You know how I would brag about you to other people. My whole life I would have given for you. Now your mother is dying and you don't even want to come see her before she dies."

All this was going through my mind and later through the minds of my father and family. Those thoughts punished me; they tore my heart out. Suddenly, life was nothing to me. But at the same time that I felt I would like to give myself up to the Lithuanian animals, the thought of that was more scary than death itself. In this mood I left the hospital without seeing my mother. To this day I don't know where her grave is.

You can understand the situation when I arrived at home. I had to deliver the news to my father and the rest of the family. I could see the thought in everyone's face as if it were spoken, "She is the lucky one. We still have to wait for our death."

As we lay down again in the attic there was nothing but dead silence. In that stillness I could hear the steady pounding of everyone's heart. We waited for death in silent panic, but also with the pain of hunger. In order to get bread we would have to stand in line with the Lithuanians. If we were recognized, however, the Germans would pick us up.

I was the only one who could go. No one paid any attention to me standing in the line. I listened to the Lithuanians while waiting. Everyone was trying to show off; this one killed more Jews than the other. They talked so cold-bloodedly that to kill a person seemed as easy as eating a piece of candy. To them, Jewish blood tasted better than the best wine. As I got my rations and started home, I saw Lithuanian partisans dragging

Jewish people, herding them. They took rabbis and their students and shaved their beards off, not with razor blades but with bits of broken glass. On some they poured gasoline and set fire to the long grey beards. I could hear them screaming to the sky, "God! God Almighty!" The Germans took photographs of this spectacle.

I also saw in the doorways and halls of Jewish homes little babies lying with heads chopped off. So many were killed each day and they were unable to remove all the bodies for burial. They couldn't hide the evidence of all the innocent bodies.

I brought my ration of bread into the kitchen downstairs where the Lithuanians were living and cut the bread so that each had a portion. Then I made tea and took it to the family in the attic. The Lithuanian and his daughter couldn't stand it. It began to bother them that so many Jews were dead but we were still there. They wanted to be rid of us, but they wanted to keep their hands clean. Why were these Jews better than any others? With us there, they could do nothing, but if we were dead they would inherit all our belongings.

The daughter decided that she would tell the Lithuanian partisans that we were hiding in the attic. Downstairs in the yard we heard a heavy knocking and the tread of boots. We huddled together as the footsteps came closer and closer. No one made a sound; we were all shivering as if in a state of shock. Soon they were outside the attic door. We heard them talking in Lithuanian, and immediately someone tore the door off the hinges and two Lithuanian partisans jumped into the room, rifles in hand, calling out, "Everyone put your hands in the air! If you try to run you will be killed immediately!"

It is hard to describe what we all felt at that moment. It took me a few seconds to move; I was paralyzed. I couldn't move a muscle and I couldn't speak. Then it came to me, "I am ready to die." As we all stood with our hands in the air, Uncle Abraham looked at the partisans and recognized one of his good friends. He began talking to him, begging him.

"What do you want from us? We didn't do anybody any harm."

My other uncles, my father, all of us begged that they shouldn't kill us. My uncle's friend softened a little, but the second man started screaming, "We have to shoot them all!"

The War Begins

Downstairs in the yard were three other partisans. We were told that if we tried to take a gun away from them the other men would come to their aid and finish us off. They were all a little drunk.

We showed them our papers to prove that we didn't belong to any Communist party, that we were born Lithuanian citizens. But they began taking people from our family. They took me, Uncle Abraham, Aunt Ettel, and Uncle Shloime and his wife Rebecca. They told us to get dressed, so we went downstairs to get some clothes. As we were walking down the steps Uncle Abraham said to the Lithuanian, "You know me. You know who I am. A long time ago you were my best friend and now you don't know me at all? You are taking me to be killed without a why or a when? Do you want money? I will give you money if you will let us go free."

The Lithuanian said, "I would let you go, but the rest of them won't. Besides, we wouldn't have come here, but you see your friends, this Lithuanian and his daughter, they came and told us you were hiding here."

They were standing there as this was said, and it was as if a bomb had been dropped on them. They had thought that we would never know how the partisans had found us.

The begging and bribing did not help. We had to get dressed and go with the Lithuanians. As we walked through the yard away from the house, my uncle said to the Lithuanians, "You won't inherit this house. I will give it to the partisans before I will leave it to you!" With those words we left our home without knowing where we were going, leaving the rest of our family behind to worry. This was one of the techniques that was used to torture the Jews, to take a few family members at a time, to drive those left behind crazy with worry and fear.

During all this my uncle's Lithuanian friend was quietly telling him, "Don't be afraid; we are not going to shoot you." We did not believe him, but in this case it was the truth.

We were taken to a school gymnasium which had a big parade field and were put on the field with many other Jewish people. We sat on benches and waited. We didn't see many women, only my two aunts. We were told to give the officials any papers we had; I had none except my birth certificate. My uncles and aunts handed in their papers. We hoped that the papers would be looked over and, if they were in order, that we would be allowed to go back home.

When it was dark, a number of Lithuanian partisans took all the men into a big room with bunk beds. Each was told to take a bed. The women were taken away separately. You can understand what kind of night we had; no one could sleep, wondering what would happen the next day. Thoughts of death came to mind, and we were anxious for the morning sun.

As the sun rose, partisans came in with black coffee, which couldn't be touched until we were dressed and washed. It was nine o'clock when the door opened and in came a civilian flanked by partisans. He looked around the room, looking everyone in the eye without saying a word. Everything was so quiet that you could hear a fly coming through. Suddenly he began talking. He introduced himself as the commander of the camp, and told us a story. He was a Lithuanian German by the name of Staikowkais. When the Russians took over Lithuania, he was working in a laundry. He photographed the Russian military bases and sent the photos to Germany; for this, he told us, he was made leader of this detention camp.

"I am not interested in keeping you all here in this camp. I am only looking for the Jewish Communists. I will go over all your papers and interrogate you. If you don't belong to the Communist party, I will let you go." That might really have happened, too, if it had not been for our Jewish women.

In the camp there was only one other teenage boy. The commandant came up to me and asked how old I was. I answered that I was sixteen. He told me that he would let me out the next morning. As I heard those words, you can understand how happy I was, but I was also worried about my uncles and aunts. I became very melancholy. I was afraid to believe it; I thought that the commandant was just making a joke—that he wouldn't release me after all.

Soon after that some Germans came in, a couple of SS men and several *Wehrmacht* members. They treated us as if we were animals, dirt. The regular soldiers looked each one of us in the eye, as if they were trying to find something. As they came to me, they stopped and told each other, "He is a real Communist."

The War Begins

The Russians were gone, so they had to find more enemies. They chose me because I was wearing a red sweater. I tried to tell them I had just gotten that sweater for a present and that it didn't have anything to do with communism, that I didn't know anything about the Communist party. As soon as they left, I took off the sweater, which in truth wasn't even red but more of a rust color. They had to find some way to make us miserable.

The whole day we had company; some Germans came in, some left. It was late and we were getting ready to sleep when a group of German soldiers, dead drunk, appeared. They sat down and told us the political news. "All the Russians are already buried. The Russian government is moving out of Moscow and in fourteen days we are going to march in the streets of Moscow."

There was a joke going around at this time. When the German army was standing before the gates of Moscow, Hitler went to the cemetery where Napoleon was buried to talk to him. He started to brag about his triumph: "See, Napoleon. You were such a great leader. You took over all of Europe. But as soon as you came to Moscow, you froze! I took all Europe and I am already twelve miles past Moscow!" Napoleon answered, "Did you go into Moscow yet?" Hitler said, "No." "Well, if not yet, then you might as well lie down next to me."

When the soldiers finished telling us all their great news, they left and we went to bed. I couldn't sleep. I tossed from one side to the other. Tomorrow morning I would be a free man again, I would see my father and the rest of my aunts and uncles. Or was it a lie? I had a heavy feeling in my heart and lay all night thinking about these things. The night seemed like a year; I couldn't wait until morning came. As soon as the sun shone through the window I climbed down from my bunk bed, washed myself, and went up to my uncles, who were lying on their bunk beds with their eyes open; there was fear in their eyes.

They told me, "Hershke, if you leave here today, go home and tell everybody not to be afraid. We are all alive and soon we will all be going home." Every hour for me was like a year, I was so nervous. With every opening of the door, every knock, I thought they were coming in to call me and tell me I could go.

The clock struck twelve, one, two, three, four and five o'clock.

It was getting dark when the door opened and in came a Lithuanian partisan with a rifle in his hand. He yelled, "Hershke Gordon, come out!" Not knowing what to do, I was so nervous, I didn't even say goodby to my uncles. I jumped up and ran to the door, and the Lithuanian partisan took me into the commandant's room.

The commandant gave me my birth certificate and told me I could go home, but he also told me to be very careful on the way so that no other Lithuanian partisans would catch me. As I was ready to leave, I remembered that I had forgotten my coat and asked the commandant if he would let me go back to pick it up. He sent me with a partisan back to the gym. So I was able to say goodby to my uncles and tell them that I hoped they would be free tomorrow.

Out on the street in the free air, I couldn't believe this was real. My heart was pounding like a hammer. I walked close to the fences to hide myself as I started home. I didn't see any civilians on the street, just here and there a few German guards. I had gone quite a way, walking slowly, step by step, when I looked up and saw the house pretty close. I started walking faster and faster. When I reached the hall, I began to breathe a little easier. I ran up the steps quickly and knocked on the door to the attic where the rest of my family was. At first I knocked very softly, not wanting to scare them, but nobody came. I knocked harder, but still no one came to open the door. I got a little angry and started knocking as hard as I could, but I understood that they must be scared stiff. I heard movement, feet scuffling and coming close to the door, but still they didn't open it. So I yelled, "Open the door! Why are you waiting?"

With a quick turn of the key the door opened and before me was Aunt Golda. She looked at me as if she was paralyzed and couldn't say one word. It was a few seconds before she jumped on me and cried out, "Hershke, Hershke, I thought you were all dead!" The rest of them heard the outcry and came running up. Nobody said a word. They all had tears in their eyes. My father took me on his lap and kissed me. Then everyone started asking questions at the same time: Where did the partisans take us? Where were the uncles and aunts? I told them everything that had happened and that I hoped maybe tomorrow or the next day all the rest of the family would come back home.

Nobody dared to believe it, but they had to, because I was the witness. They made me something to eat and, as soon as I finished eating, I fell asleep right at the table. The next morning, my uncles began telling me what they had been through with the Lithuanian hired hand and his daughter after we were taken. At noon we heard a strong knock at the door—not just one, but a couple of knocks. We thought it was the Lithuanian partisans, so again everyone panicked, but it didn't help; we had to look death in the eye. My father went to the door, opened it quickly, and there was the same picture as yesterday—my two aunts and Uncle Abraham were back home. Only Shloime was still left in the camp. You can understand the happiness we felt at being all together again. Uncle Abraham told us how he got out of the camp.

The commandant had called him into the office and tried to interrogate him, at which time my uncle and the commandant were alone. My uncle told him, "You know very well that I am not a Communist. You saw that in all the papers I gave you. The women, they are not Communists either. Why should you have us in this camp? Why should you keep us here when we haven't done anything? Why make us miserable? If you want some money, I will give you some money."

The commandant didn't even blink an eye; he pretended that he hadn't heard. Uncle Abraham was wearing a gold watch, which he took off and put on the table for the commandant. As soon as the commandant saw the watch, his eyes shone. Looking around the room to make sure no one could see, he took the watch, put it in his pocket and said, "All right, I'll let you go—you, your wife and the other woman—but your brother-in-law I can't release yet; it would be too many at once. Tomorrow I will let him go. Send his wife to pick him up."

So it went. Everyone who bribed a little he let go, but he couldn't let everyone go at the same time or it would look suspicious. The Lithuanian commandant himself was afraid that if the Germans found out that he was being bribed into letting people go, they would take care of him, too. All the women with husbands who weren't there at the same time as the others got together and formed a group. They went to the German commandant to complain about the Lithuanian commandant taking diamonds and gold and money. The German commandant immediately took trucks with military men out to the camp and took away whatever women and men were left, as well as the Lithuanian commandant, to be shot. Thus my youngest uncle was killed.

This was our second fatality. Our family was getting smaller, becoming more broken. Everyone was thinking that, even if there were a miracle and we were all left alive, we would never see those two again. Aunt Rebecca left us, too, to stay with some relatives. That left my father and myself, Uncle Abraham and Aunt Ettel, Uncle Borach and Aunt Celia and their son, and Uncle Yenchik, Aunt Golda, and their two children.

4. The Purge of Slobodka

Slobodka was a suburb of Kovno, connected to it by a bridge. It was at that time the home of the pious, strict Jews, the important rabbis and students of the Torah. Many scholars came from there. When you mentioned Slobodka, the name rang all over the world. It was identified with the *Yeshivot* (the Orthodox rabbinical schools) from which came very scholarly men, well-versed in the Talmud and the Torah. Approximately 6,000 Jews lived there, integrated with the Lithuanians. Most were working men—shoemakers, tailors, and butchers.

On Wednesday, June 25, at 7:00 PM the purge started. Large gangs of Lithuanian partisans began throwing all the Jews out of their houses. When they had a big group of women, children, and men, they put them in rows and told them to run to the river. As they came to the river, there were more gangs of Lithuanian partisans with machine guns who told everyone to take off all their clothes and run into the lake. As they ran into the lake, they were machine gunned. This continued for two days.

When we heard about the purge, we were worried about the people we knew there. It was decided that I would sneak over and find out what had happened. Many people had been killed right in their homes. I went into one house where the floor was covered with blood. Two cut-off legs lay in one room and in another there was a mutilated body. The severed head of the body was resting on the table in the kitchen with two needles in the eyes. In a second home, I found a family of five, all with their tongues protruding and blue; they had been choked to death. In a third house there was a family of six: a mother, a father, and four little children. They had been nailed to the table with large nails. Before they died, as they tried to fight the murderers off, they had had enough time to write in Yiddish, in their own blood, on the walls and the floor, "Any brothers or sisters who survive, take revenge for our spilled and innocent blood."

The morning after the purge began, the Lithuanian partisans started catching Jews to take away the dead bodies because it was warm and they were afraid of epidemics. They were told to dig big graves in back of the town, where they buried all the bodies, 700 to 1,000 Jews. A week after this purge the water in the gutters was still red with Jewish blood. In the river, you could see the bodies wash up onto the shore all day.

A very good friend of ours, Pohoch Melamed, lived in Slobodka. We thought that for sure she had been killed. But one sunny morning she dressed herself as a girl from the farm and came to our house to see us. We didn't believe it; we thought she had come back from the dead. She told us that on the night of the purge, she thought that she would go crazy. She survived because of the help of a Lithuanian. Next to her house there lived a very nice Lithuanian fellow. When he found out what the partisans were doing to the Jews, he was hurt. He had been brought up with Jewish people. He stood all night in the hall of her house until the purge was over. As Lithuanian partisans came up, they would ask if there were any Jews. He would say, "There are no Jews living here, no need to look; there are no Jews in here." Since their own kind told them, they believed him. In this way the whole family was left alive. Of such men there were very few; you could count them on your fingers.

After the purge, the Lithuanians and the Germans were drunk on Jewish blood. They began thinking of ways to get all the Jews who were left in one place—a ghetto so that any time they needed Jews to kill, they wouldn't have to look for them. They also wanted to isolate the Jews from the Lithuanians. They decided that the ghetto would be in Slobodka. Since there were still some Lithuanians living in the area they had designated, the Germans allowed the Lithuanians to trade homes with Jews. Thus we ended up having to bargain with the Lithuanian janitor who had turned us in to the partisans hoping to inherit

The Purge of Slobodka

our house free and clear. We made a contract that we would live in his house in Slobodka, but that after the war, if we were alive, each would go back to his own home.

The Jews were already impatiently waiting for the order from the Gestapo to move to the ghetto. Many of the Jews thought that if we went to the ghetto they would leave us alone, that they would let us sit there until after the war was over. That was a big mistake.

On July 10 the Gestapo gave the order for all Jews to move into the ghetto by the fifteenth of August. By the next morning, signs were posted on all streets and corners that any Jews caught living with Lithuanians after that would be shot on the spot, and so it was done.

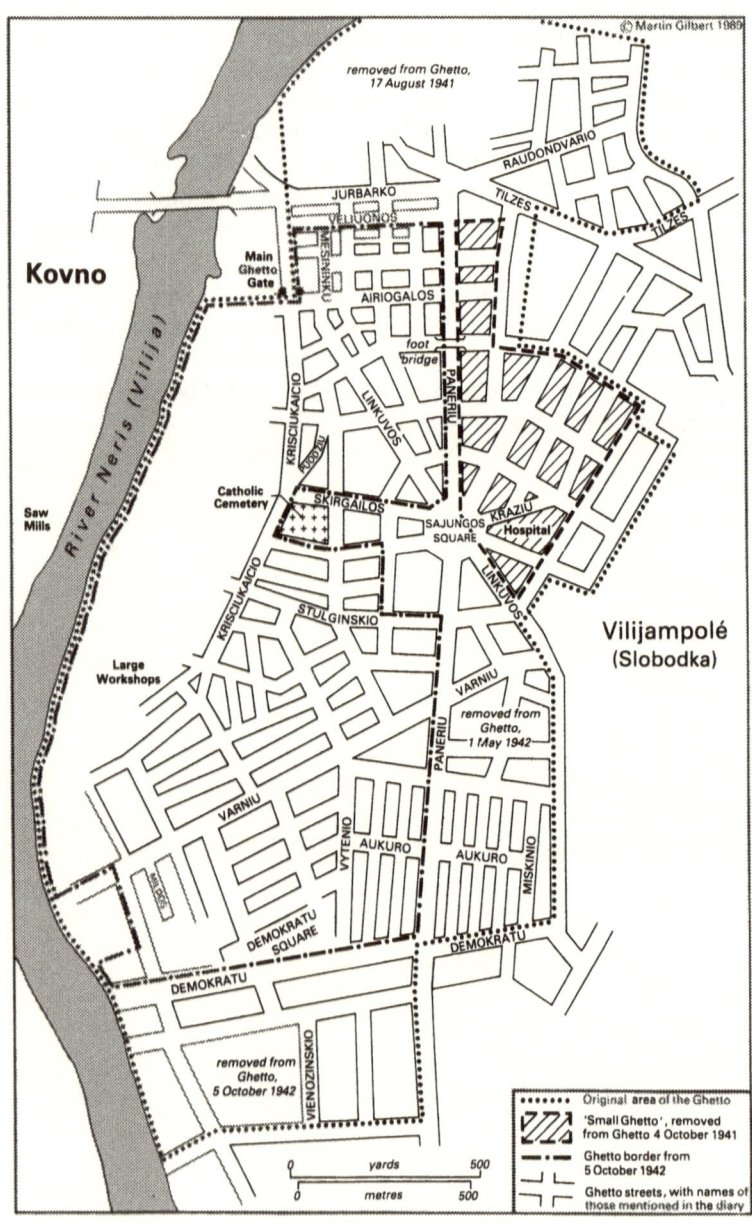

The Kovno Ghetto: streets and boundaries

5. Moving to the Ghetto

The moving of the Jews to the ghetto started in the middle of the week. The sky was covered with very small white clouds through which the sun's rays beamed brightly. Our community started to move as soon as the order was issued. We could see caravans of disheartened men, women, and children. They were still alive but their faces were dead. Everyone carried on his shoulders whatever he could; those who were more prosperous rented a cart or wagon and horse from the Lithuanians to move all their belongings. Those who could afford to rent a wagon and horse didn't have to worry so much; they could take all their necessities. But people who couldn't afford it took only the bare essentials. This caused some jealousy among the Jews. One would say, "Look who's riding, taking his belongings in a wagon. I have to walk and take only what I can carry on my shoulders." It wasn't that way; people with horses and wagons took other people on, but there wasn't enough space for all. Some Jews who were dragging their things called out loudly, "Hey! Look at his horse. They are sure to live through the war, but I won't even make it alive to the ghetto! I can only take a little; I have to leave all my belongings to the Lithuanian murderers." Some took all their furniture and some did not, but a little later the Germans came into the ghetto and took all the furniture anyway. There was a saying about jealousy at this time: "As long as you are alive, your eyes are very big, even when death is waiting on the tip of your nose."

Since my grandfather's wagons and horses had been nationalized, we rented a wagon and horse to take what we could to the ghetto. We packed everything that would fit, but we took no furniture. When the wagon was loaded, we sat on top of our belongings—all of us on top of the wagon, my father and myself, three uncles and three aunts and three cousins. When we reached the bridge that crossed to Slobodka, two German SS men with a few Lithuanian partisans came up to us and told the driver of the wagon to stop. They told us all to get down, stand in a line, and keep our hands in the air. They looked us over from top to bottom and told us they needed volunteer workmen. They wanted someone to work voluntarily, but if they had to, they would choose and take by force. Among us there was a dead stillness. Everyone was so scared that they broke into a sweat, trembling. Nobody said a word or volunteered.

When they saw that no one was volunteering, they pulled out my father. He begged them, crying, telling them how my mother died in the first days of the war and without him I would be alone. All this begging didn't help. They took him with a jerk and pulled him away, not even letting him say goodby to me or the rest of the family. Where they were taking him no one knew. I saw him only one more time, in the concentration camp at Dachau. But that is a chapter for later.

Suddenly I was alone, even with the rest of the family around me. I felt so empty and miserable. Uncle Abraham and Aunt Ettel had always loved me like a son, and as soon as the Germans took my father away they took me under their wings as if I was their own; but they didn't know how to console me. The rest of the uncles and aunts also tried, but all this care and sympathy couldn't make up for a mother and father. When I had had both parents, I had taken them for granted; but, as they say, when you don't have it, it is then that you really appreciate what you had.

6. In the Ghetto

The ghetto fences were locked and no one could leave at all. There were a lot of people who didn't have any rooms to move into, so many people were lying in the streets and many families were living all together in one room. But the Jews didn't lose hope. Everybody thought this was not for long, that we would be left alive over our murderers. All our Jewish politicians (everybody became a politician) became colossal optimists. Everyone would tell you what you wanted to hear. Each was trying to cheer you up and to cheer himself up.

There were two ghettos behind the fences, a little one and a big one, connected by a bridge, and about 30,000 Jews. On the bridge was a Lithuanian with a gun. We could walk from the big to the little ghetto only between 6:00 AM and 8:00 PM. If anyone was seen after 9:00 PM outside his house, he was shot to death on the spot. The fence surrounding the ghetto had electric wiring so that if anybody tried to run he would be electrocuted. On the other side of the ghetto fence there were Lithuanian partisans and German guards every five meters with big searchlights.

We lived in the little ghetto at 27 Paneriu Street, which was close to the fence. Every morning Lithuanian partisans and Germans came into the ghetto to catch people to work. After work they would bring them back, some still able to walk, others beaten up and bloody. The catching of men to work took several hours. This we knew because we were close to the fence. In these hours we would hide in the attic. When we saw that they had gotten enough people, we would come down from the attic and wait for night.

Nearly every night, around 1:00 AM, the guards would start shooting. They kept pounding and shooting just to keep us in panic, to keep us scared so we wouldn't know what to think or be able to get together and organize to rebel, to make a stand against the Germans. And so it was; all this fear kept us disoriented—it didn't even occur to us to fight back. The only thing we could feel was the terror that we would soon be dead.

The Germans came to the conclusion that they shouldn't have to run every day to catch Jews to work. They decided they would create a Jewish government, a Jewish Presidium of elders and Jewish police who would be responsible to the Germans. They would tell them that they wanted 500 Jews to work and the Jewish government would be responsible for delivering 500 people. The man chosen as chairman was Dr. Elkes, a very intelligent, a very honorable man. He was assisted by five others. Yakov Goldberg was head of the labor office and Pavel Margolis was in charge of recruiting workers. The better positions went to the family and friends of these officials.

This group started the Jewish police for the ghetto. The Germans knew that if they gave these particular people a little more food they would be able to get anything out of them, whether information or getting them to do whatever they wanted them to do. And that was the way it was.

The Germans also began to organize stores in the ghetto—not places where you could buy anything, but more like factories where things were made and distributed. Each Jew got a ration card. We went to the stores, showed our card, and got our rations for the week: a four pound loaf of bread, two and a half ounces of salad, a pound of horsemeat, and, once a month, a little marmalade. They would bring in the dead horses shot at the front line and prepare them in the ghetto.

In short, the Germans built a little Jewish state. Nobody believed, even the Jewish government and police, that the Germans would leave it to them to rule the whole ghetto. The Germans, however, understood what they were doing.

All over the ghetto, the police went from one house to another to register everyone. All of the lists with names and numbers of people were given to the Germans. Using those lists the Germans would send in just enough food and decide how many Jews they wanted delivered to work. The Jewish police delivered to the Germans exactly the number of people needed, rounding them up any way they could, beating and kicking those who didn't want to go. They were living well while the rest of us were either running around confused or trying to hide ourselves to stay out of the way of the work patrols. It wasn't long before the Jewish police had an opportunity to profit even more from our misery.

7. The Collection of Valuables

We had hoped to hold onto what little property we had, but at the beginning of September an order appeared that all valuables must be delivered to the Jewish council on September 4, under an order from the Germans. After that the Gestapo would come with bloodhounds and go from house to house looking for any hidden valuables. If they found any at all, they would shoot not only everyone in the household but everyone on the whole block. It was the middle of the week. The sky was covered with dark clouds and that was how everyone felt at the time. Everyone was scared, not so much about himself as that maybe his brother or neighbor would try to hide something.

The Jewish police went all over the ghetto trying to tell everyone not to hide anything but to give it up voluntarily. Each block had a depository and everyone went to it to give up everything he had. There were long lines with each person holding something in his hands—his wife's diamond or a gold watch, or carrying a fur coat on his shoulder. On everyone's face one could read, "Maybe this is going to help. We have given up everything we have. Maybe this will buy our lives." On the other hand, everyone was thinking, "Look at these things, at the fur coat I have worked hard for, and now I have to give it to the murderers. But if I could buy my life. . . ." It really meant nothing. Today the valuables, tomorrow our lives.

When we moved to the ghetto, my uncles and aunts buried all their valuables in the garage. They took a sheet metal bathtub and dug a hole under the pile of firewood, placed all their furs and valuables in the tub, and buried it, covering it with the

The Collection of Valuables

firewood. When the order came, we had to take all the firewood off again, uncover the tub, and take it all to the murderers. My aunts were screaming and crying, not so much because of the worth of the gold and diamonds as because of the sentimental value. When Aunt Ettel had married, Uncle Abraham had given her a brooch, earrings, and a diamond wedding ring; but my uncle said to her, "If you are going to be alive you will have other jewels and fur coats, but if you are not going to be alive, what good are the diamonds and furs?" His words didn't help, for she was still crying.

The aunts discussed the situation, saying, "Why did we even dig it up? The Germans were not going to find it anyway." For a while it seemed that we were going to bury it again, but the uncles said no, that we were going to give it all to the Germans, and that's the way it was done.

I went to the depository carrying a box that held my aunts' diamond rings or some other valuables. I didn't know what was in it for sure, but it seemed to weigh a few pounds. Uncle Abraham was carrying the fur coats. As we came to the depository, we got in line and from the side saw Jewish police standing to keep order. I kept staring at the box; it was bothering me that I would soon have to give the box to the Germans. We saw that the Jewish police took some things from people standing in line, saying that they would take it to the depository, but instead of turning it in, as they went through the back door of the depository they would put it in their pockets. They took the valuables from their brothers to their own homes and hid them. Their homes were not searched by the Germans.

We were surprised that there were no German guards, only Jews. As we approached the depository, there was a thin older Jewish man sitting by a little table who wrote down whatever was turned in and gave each person a receipt. Inside the depository Jewish police walked around whispering to each other. For them it was just like Christmas in the United States. As Uncle Abraham and I left the depository with a piece of paper in our hands, we did not say a word to each other; we just looked at each other and went home.

When we came into the house, the aunts gave us resentful looks, but they were quiet. They wanted us to talk, but we didn't say anything either. That silence must have held for at least a half an hour, until Aunt Golda jumped up with a question: "Well, did the Germans search you in the depository?" Uncle Abraham answered, "In the depository there were no Germans, only our own Jews who took our gold and everything away from us. Here is the piece of paper they gave us."

Aunt Golda spoke with a harsh voice, "You see? I told you before—I hope that I am lying—that that was only to scare us so we would give everything up right away. The Jewish police wanted our valuables. I'll bet you the Germans won't even come to search our houses and I'll bet you that the one who hides his valuables will have a lot easier life in the ghetto, not like us, the stupid ones. We went and dug it up from the ground and gave it right to the devil in his hands. Even if the Germans do come, they wouldn't ever have found it. But now it is too late. Why should I eat my heart out? It's too late. It is all done."

Everybody sat very quietly with a hangdog look, heads down. Nobody had any words to answer. I could tell that the uncles felt sorry and knew they had made a mistake. Later on it really showed; those who had all their valuables hidden lived pretty well because they could bribe their way out of being sent to work outside the ghetto.

After three days, German SS men came with bloodhounds, looking for valuables. Half the ghetto had hidden their valuables but only a few families were found out. Those families were executed in their homes. While the Germans were looking for valuables, if they saw nice furniture, they would tell people to put it onto the street. Then big trucks pulled up and took it to the houses where the Germans lived.

When my uncles heard that the dogs were running around searching for valuables, they felt better, but my Aunt Golda didn't talk about valuables any more. We knew that she felt in her heart that we had made a mistake.

When the collection was over, life in the ghetto became again as before, with the Jewish police catching people to work. But

The Collection of Valuables

this didn't last long. The Germans wanted to see how the Jews would react if they tried to pull people out of the ghetto and kill them. They wanted to see if the Jews would fight or just go like sheep to the slaughter.

8. The First Practice Massacre

September 17, 1941, was a sunny but cold morning, and the roofs were covered with a thin layer of frost. We were still in our beds when we heard on the street past the fence the marching of Lithuanian partisans singing the Lithuanian national anthem. The tramping of boots and the singing scared us to death. Everyone was afraid to look through the window to see where they were going. We thought it sounded as if they were going past the fence but it also sounded as if they were walking in the streets of the ghetto. Uncle Abraham said to us, "The Germans are sending the partisans to the Russian front. That's why they are so happy and singing."

When we could hear no more singing, we quieted down and went back to sleep. Suddenly, we heard a loud knock at the door. I jumped down from my bed and ran to the door and asked, "Who is it?" From the other side of the door I heard a woman's voice; it was our neighbor, Meryl.

"Hey, it is 7:00 AM. What do you want? Everybody is sleeping."

"Wake them up," she told me. "The ghetto is surrounded by Lithuanians and Germans and on the top of the bridge there are Lithuanians and Germans with machine guns."

I woke everyone up and we got dressed in a cold shiver; nobody ate or drank anything, and we stood waiting for whatever would happen next. Every once in a while someone from our immediate family would go out into the yard and look through a hole in the fence to see if any Lithuanians or Germans were running through the ghetto. We knew that today would bring no good.

The First Practice Massacre

We heard, from a little farther away, yelling and running. All over the little ghetto, Germans and Lithuanians were trying to throw everybody out of their houses, making them run toward the bridge. Can you imagine the hollering, screaming, and crying from the children, the women, the men? The door of our house flew open and two Germans with two partisans with guns in their hands told us to run toward the bridge. They ran into our house and looked for anyone hiding. At the same time, the Lithuanian partisans started taking whatever they could see of value. When we came back from that massacre, the whole house was turned upside down. All our belongings were on the floor and everything was a mess. When we put everything back in order, we found we were missing quite a few things.

When they told us to run toward the bridge, we thought, "The end is near." Approaching the bridge, we stood in lines by families. As we walked along in the rows, a lot of people started saying prayers, saying goodby, and shaking hands with each other. When we came closer to the bridge there were Germans from the Gestapo who had big heavy rubber clubs in their hands. They let everyone have it right over the head or wherever they could hit as we came by in the line. They didn't let anyone through without a hit.

The Gestapo sorted out the Jews as if we were animals. They looked at our teeth to see how old we were, how we looked, how tall we were. They put older people in one line, younger people in another, and children in a third. They took me from my aunts and uncles and put me with my age group and took us away. As they took us, I was thinking that I had no one anymore. What was I going to do? I was altogether like a dead man, alone, like a stone. Tears poured from my eyes. I was talking to myself. "I wish they had already shot me. I wouldn't have to go through this misery again."

In the little ghetto there was a children's hospital used only for newborn babies. In the large ghetto they had a hospital for the sick. The Germans gave an order that there were not to be any more babies born in the ghetto, that the children's hospital was for the babies conceived before the order came into effect and for orphaned infants.

It was to the children's hospital that they took us now, into the nursery where the newborn babies were. To me, at that time, they looked like little monkeys, very undernourished, screaming; they looked very hungry. One Lithuanian told us to each take a baby and go back to the place where all the groups were. We were children ourselves; we didn't know how to handle babies like this; we could very easily hurt a little hand or leg. But who paid any attention to how we carried the babies? Nobody knew what part of the world we were in.

Even though I didn't know what was happening, I tried to comfort the little baby as much as I could. I was smart enough to remember to take a cover from the bed to wrap him in. I bundled him up and put him under my arm. As we ran down from the hospital we were again counted to make sure each one was there. We were put in a line and told to go back to the place where everyone else was standing, waiting for their fortune.

I looked for my uncles and aunts, but there was such a crowd that I couldn't see them. Germans were running around with clubs hitting people. I gave up and stood there waiting like everyone else. On one side were the Lithuanians with loaded rifles, ready to shoot. Above there were German planes taking pictures, and that was not a stupid idea, because if they lost the war, they would have to answer to the world. After this was over, the world would start asking questions. "What happened to the whole of European Jewry? Why did you kill so many people? They didn't declare war on you; they were only the civilian population." Then the Germans would take out the pictures and say, "We didn't do anything. The Lithuanians did all the killing." But the Germans told them to do it.

On one side I saw the Germans drive up with big trucks in which they put the old people and the little babies. They pushed the people in and threw the little babies in like sacks of potatoes. They took them away. The other people my age gave up their babies, and the screaming of the babies and the cries of the older people could tear the skies apart. Some children wouldn't give the babies up but ran into the truck with them. No one knew if the trucks were good or bad. As all this was going on I kept my baby under my arm, not giving it up. I didn't know if he was alive or dead. I looked under the cover to see, and the baby was getting a yellowish color. A woman standing behind me told me, "Look how you are holding the baby, like you are carrying a suitcase." I turned around and said, "I'm sorry. I never had the opportunity to handle one like this before. I don't know how to hold him."

Even though my head was occupied with many different thoughts, I would take a look occasionally to see how the baby was. As I looked at the baby, I felt helpless with compassion. I felt that he would never be able to take it—no food, the cold; nobody knew how long we would have to stand there and wait for our number to be up. Suddenly an automobile appeared and two German Gestapo jumped out and started to talk to the Gestapo already there, all whispering to each other. After about ten minutes the German and Lithuanian guards began yelling and pushing the Jews back toward the ghetto. The whole practice massacre had lasted five hours.

On the other side of the bridge, in the big ghetto, the people were standing by, looking at what was happening. The people there were watching, ready to go to their deaths too, for everybody knew that what happened to the little ghetto would also happen to the big one. The Jews from the big ghetto, even though they weren't in the same place, went through the same fear of death, the same thoughts.

As we started to run back home, you can understand what a relief overcame everyone. The running was abnormal, as was the crying and the screaming from the women and children. Until then everyone had been as if dead, but now they started crying hysterically. The trucks with the old people and children were brought back. It was like a miracle that the Jews had all been spared from death so far. Right away the very religious Jews, the Orthodox, said, "See, this is our God. He has created a miracle." They also said to the non-Orthodox Jews that if they had gone to the synagogue maybe all this trouble wouldn't have happened. The optimists started talking. "See, I think that Hitler must have gotten beaten somewhere with the Russians." Everybody thought that the war was almost over and Hitler was dead, that we could soon go back home and wouldn't have to remain in the ghetto. This was all an illusion. The Germans had found that they would have no trouble with the Jews; their work could be done smoothly and efficiently. There would be no rebellions.

I ran back to the ghetto with the baby still fast under my arm. I made sure that I didn't lose him in all that commotion, with each person pushing another. As I was running, I looked at him every minute to see whether his eyes were open or closed. I was convinced that that little baby for sure wasn't going to make it through. Back home, I found my uncles and aunts. When everyone saw me coming in with a baby under my arm, they began crying and laughing hysterically. As we came to our senses, each told his story of what had happened. I told where they had taken me and where they told me to take the baby. Aunt Ettel made some food for the baby. As he finished eating, she wrapped him in a nice warm cover and put him in bed. We could see that the baby was getting back his natural color, and a smile even appeared on his face. I wasn't so scared when I realized that the baby would live. When the baby felt better, I took him back to the children's hospital. Walking there I met the older people whom the Germans had just returned in the trucks.

I talked to them and asked where the Germans had taken them. They told me they had been taken to a medieval fort that the Germans had modernized with machine guns, the Ninth Fort. In our country there were quite a few such forts from past wars, built with high walls and tunnels for protection, and soldiers would pour down hot tar from the top of the walls while their enemies shot at the wall with heavy stones.

The next morning after the practice massacre, the Germans and Lithuanians started catching people to go to work again, not using the lists because a lot of people were not in their homes or were hiding. The Jewish police and Germans ran along the streets and in the houses, pulling people out.

9. The Airfield Work Brigade

When the Germans started the war with the Russians, they bombarded the airfield with the Russian planes, completely destroying it. Now the Germans wanted to repair the fields for their own use, so they would be able to land, fuel up, and take off again. Where do you think they got the manpower? The Jews from the ghetto. The work was very hard, and we were gone seventeen or eighteen hours a day.

Every morning about a thousand people marched out from the ghetto under the guard of the Wehrmacht. The road from the ghetto to the airport was about eight miles long. The guards walked on the sidewalks while we walked on the stone streets, six or eight abreast.

At the same time that we were marching in the streets, the Lithuanians were walking on the sidewalks going to work. They would laugh at us and insult us in Lithuanian, so all the Jews walked with their heads lowered. We wore the yellow star of David in front and back. The star had to be sewn on tight, with no loose ends. If it was only pinned on, we would be shot. But a lot of Jews used to take the risk; these we called rabbits. As soon as we got a mile or two outside the ghetto and had a chance to mingle with the Lithuanians, these rabbits would take off the star in front and ask the man in back to take off the back one for them so they could escape. They loved going on the airfield brigade because it gave them a better chance to escape. As soon as both stars were off, they waited for the right moment to jump out and mix with the Lithuanians and disappear. This was a deadly game. If the guards caught them, they were shot right there, no questions asked. It had to be done very quickly so that neither the Germans nor the walking Lithuanians could see. They really had to work at it. There was no chance to look back or hesitate.

Even though they were playing with their lives, every morning there would be quite a few rabbits like this. Many had Lithuanian friends to whom they would go and be fed: butter, bread, and ham (which Jews weren't supposed to eat, but at that time we would eat anything if you could just have enough to eat). There were other Lithuanians who didn't want to have anything to do with the rabbits and would turn them and their Lithuanian friends in to the Gestapo.

When we arrived at the airfield, we were already tired from walking, but then we had to go to work. There were German foremen who wore uniforms but weren't guards, and they ran things. There were quite a few of them and each would take some people, fifty to a hundred, to work. There were big holes in the runway which we had to fill with sand, then we had to pave the whole airfield with cement. We had to unload carloads of cement and help put up barracks for the German Air Force.

At the same place where we were working, across from us, the Russian prisoners were working. Their guards were the Hitler Youth, the youngsters who belonged to the Hitler organization; the oldest were perhaps seventeen. Each one wore brown boots and a brown coat with a swastika on the left arm and carried a rifle and a little bayonet. They were egotistical brats, or, as we called them, "monsters." How they treated the Russian prisoners is hard to describe. These little brats killed hundreds of Russians every day. They were twenty feet away and we could see that they were helpless, so tired that they were as weak as flies. Their rations were a lot lower than ours.

When they were close enough, they would call to us in Russian, "Give us some bread, we want to eat." Many of them would try to get over to our group. Some told us that they were Jews also and to bring some clothes the next day so they could change from their uniforms and go back with us to the ghetto, since it was worse where they were. A lot of Jews did bring clothes and took the Russians into the ghetto. There were many Jews who were prisoners in the Russian army, and the Russians of different ethnic groups told the Germans who the Jews were in the hope of getting extra food for informing. As soon as the Germans found out about it and caught a Jewish Russian changing his clothes, they would shoot him right there.

I remember one little monster who looked to me not older than fifteen. He had with him twenty-five Russians who were carrying ten concrete bricks each. You could see that they were moving slowly, undernourished and weak. That little monster was going around telling them to run, not walk. You could see that they were trying but they couldn't. He got mad and took a shovel and started hitting everyone on the head. It didn't take long until all twenty-five men were dead. Right away other Russians came with primitive stretchers, picked up the bodies, and carried them away to a hole, dropped them in, and covered them up.

Every now and then we could see two Russians dragging a stretcher with four or five dead on it. As we worked, we were getting beaten too, but the Russians were getting worse treatment. We were beaten by the German foremen and engineers, and a lot of our people had to be carried back to the ghetto on stretchers, but at least they did not beat us to death.

When we started home after the day's work, we began to feel a little happier. We would get in lines so they could count us to see if everyone was there. They never came up with the right number; sometimes it was more, sometimes less. The counting took an hour or so extra. Going home, we would go a little faster than going to work. Even though we were tired, as soon as we started for the ghetto we would find some strength. We didn't walk; we ran. As we came nearer the Slobodka bridge not far from the ghetto, our lines filled up with the rabbits who were coming back home for the night and, as they came in, the lines got wider. Many had food in knapsacks on their backs.

Since the lines were not supposed to be more than eight abreast, the guards would run up and ask, "Where do you come from?" Someone had to move back. People didn't want to be pushed back, so they would argue about who would go back. They didn't want to relinquish their places to the rabbits. They would begin fighting as they walked, elbowing each other to keep their places. When a man was very tired and a guy jumped in with all kinds of food, he would sometimes get so mad that he would go to the guard and tell him that a rabbit had come in.

Why was it like this? Everyone wanted to be the first one back. A thousand people had to go through the gate one by one to be searched, which took a long time. No one wanted to be the last one through. Many Jews would say, "Hey, look. He's carrying a whole knapsack of food and now I have to give him my place. Of course, if he wants to give me some of his food. . . ." Jealousy toward the rabbits grew more bitter, even though the rabbit risked his own life for the food. One Jew saw that another Jew had a little more bread, and he would say, "I wish he were dead."

And so it went. We began to fall into a routine and forget about what the Germans were planning. We just wanted to get through another day. But it didn't take long for the Germans to carry out their first mass execution.

10. The Liquidation of the Little Ghetto

Saturday, October 4, 1941. The ground was covered with a silvery coating of snow and the sky was overcast with grayish clouds. The whole city around the ghetto was still in a deep sleep. The little ghetto was surrounded by Germans, Lithuanian partisans, and Ukrainians who had joined the Germans when they took over part of Russia. Before we had time to get dressed there were soldiers in our neighborhood. We didn't even have a chance to get our coats before we ran out into the street. They told us to get in line by families. I got in line with Uncle Abraham and Aunt Ettel, Aunt Golda and Uncle Yenchik and their two children (Aunt Golda held the little boy in her arms), Aunt Celia and Uncle Borach and their boy, Maishke. As soon as we were all in line, they told us to start running forward. In front of us was a Lithuanian who showed us the way to run. We ran past the bridge from the big ghetto and turned back to the place where we had stood in the practice massacre. As we came to the place, there were already many people there and every minute more and more came. Two men came dragging a sick woman on a stretcher. We could see other people dragging the paralyzed, bringing the retarded and invalids and people without arms or legs. Mothers were running with their babies in their arms, tearing their hair out. By the children's hospital they had seen Jewish men digging graves. What this all meant no one could understand, but everyone was still trying to be optimistic. Everyone hoped this would be like the first time, that they would punish us for a couple of hours and then tell us to go back home. But this wasn't to be like the first time.

Before long the whole population of the little ghetto was standing in the field by the bridge, waiting to learn their fate. We could see in the middle of the field a dais, a small stage about six feet square. On that stage was a little SS man from the Gestapo with the name of Rauca. He looked fat, like a pig, and you could see the murder in his face.

Suddenly an order came for each family to pass in line in front of Rauca. They were starting to sort. The first ones to march by were the Jewish police, four abreast, wearing dark uniforms and shiny black boots. They went by just like the military, everyone in step. Rauca liked that and pointed his finger to the right. This finger indicated the decision between life and death. We realized that the police were on the side to live, the right-hand side.

As soon as the police had marched by, they began, together with the Lithuanians, Ukrainians, and Germans, to help make order in the lines. People were confused, running one way and another. The soldiers made use of this by hitting people over the head. They hit so hard that some of them broke their rifles. Our Jewish police were kicking with their boots, which hurt too. During this time people continued marching past the platform and watching the sign of the finger, right, left, right, left—life or death. Uncle Abraham and the rest of the family decided that we would not rush but would let all the others march ahead.

As the day went on, the picture became more gruesome. The Gestapo leader started tearing families apart, sending the men one way, the women and children another. The men wanted to run to their wives and the wives to their husbands, and as they did the Lithuanian, German, and Ukrainian soldiers started shooting. The screaming of the women and children could have torn stones apart.

It began to get dark, so we decided we would march by the dais. It is hard to explain the feeling as we walked past. Would it be right or left? We went without thinking, mindless, numb. We were getting closer and closer to the platform. The dread of which way he would point was unbearable.

Here there occurred a miracle. For the whole party of us, eight or ten lines of people, including my family, he pointed to the right. Our fate was to stay alive and suffer. All the people who had been sent to the left side were taken by the soldiers to the Ninth Fort to be shot. In the little ghetto there had been five thousand Jews; two thousand of them were killed. The Germans took the rest of us over to the big ghetto.

Marching to the big ghetto, we could see that the children's hospital was in flames. I heard from friends and other Jewish people in the big ghetto that the Germans had given an order that day for all the Jewish doctors and nurses to go to the children's hospital. All the doors of the hospital were locked and the Germans and Ukrainians then poured gasoline over the building and set it on fire. People said that one doctor tried to break through a window and jump, but as he did so a German guard shot and killed him in the air. You can understand how we all felt. But, as the saying goes, "The dead ones don't eat anything, but the living ones still hope."

On the way to the big ghetto, as we met friends or families who were still alive, we would hug and kiss each other because we were still alive. This was especially true after we met with friends who lived in the big ghetto and had wondered if we would survive. Here we met our very good friend Genya Nechmud. She was my mother's best friend. They had gone to school together and were brought up like sisters. In the good times, she used to come to our house almost every day. When she saw us, she felt such joy and excitement that she fainted. After she revived, the first words that tumbled out were, "Let's go to our house. We will have something to eat."

We no longer had a house, and for us this was a miracle. If it weren't for our good friend we would have had to sleep in the street and go without food. As we entered her house, we met her husband and children, and everyone hugged and kissed each other, crying hysterically—not just the women but even the men. The tears were very bitter, like little children. After we had all calmed down, they set the table and brought us some food, but nobody could eat anything. Everyone's heart was burdened. Each took a couple of bites of a piece of bread but could not eat more. I think we wanted sleep more than food.

The whole Nechmud family understood that; they gave us

their beds and they slept on the floor. These were the kind of people who would give you the shirts off their backs. As soon as we got into bed, we fell asleep and did not wake until eleven o'clock the next morning. While we dressed and washed, they prepared food for us. They didn't want us to do anything to help in the house. When we told them that we must leave and look for a place to stay, they didn't want to hear of it, but we understood that it wasn't possible for all of us to live in such a small house.

My uncles and aunts walked through the big ghetto to look for relations or friends who might have a little more room to spare. Uncle Yenchik found his sister Meenah, and she took him in, with Golda and their children. Uncle Borach Shapiro, Aunt Celia, and Maishke moved in with his brother-in-law, Yankel Verboski. Uncle Abraham and Aunt Ettel and I went to my uncle's best friend, Shia Yet. Our family was divided. We lived at 67 Dwary Gatvia, Uncle Yenchik at Krisciukaicio Gatvia number 10, and Uncle Borach Shapiro at 57 Paneriu Gatvia.

11. Life in the Big Ghetto

The displacement to the big ghetto started a new life and new troubles for us. The Germans had taken us from the small ghetto without even a shirt. Even though life was miserable, one still needed a bed, a shirt, and socks, a pan to cook with. We had to go to our friends, to borrow from anyone who had a little extra. We had left our house in the little ghetto with only what we had on, and now had to go to our friends and beg. A lot of people didn't have to be asked. They knew and came offering help. But there were also people, even friends and relations, who, when we came asking for something, didn't want anything to do with us. The situation of those who came from the small ghetto was very difficult, and the sanitary conditions were deplorable.

My uncle and aunt were sleeping on a bunk bed in a little place that looked like a chicken coop out back of the house. It had a small kitchen where I slept on two chairs. I had no place to stretch out my feet, so I would put them on the window sill. The kitchen was only as big as a yawn. We didn't have any blankets with which to cover ourselves.

The situation became more depressing. Before, when we were in the little ghetto, we thought the war wasn't going to last long, but here we lost hope. We had the feeling that nobody would be left alive.

Day in, day out, I went to work at the airfield. All the men in the ghetto were sent to work. I couldn't wait to get back home at night. There I would find the *joshnik* cooking. It was a soup made of stinking horsemeat, already half rotten. That ration of horsemeat was supposed to last a week, but with three people like us it lasted for two meals. The meatballs my aunt would make from the horsemeat could be smelled a mile away, but we ate them with quite an appetite. We were so hungry it tasted as good as chicken meat. When I finished eating, I would still be hungry, so I would go to my Aunt Golda's. Whenever I came to her house she would give me something to eat, and I would make sure that I came when they were eating. As soon as I came in she would ask me, "What do you want first, the soup or the meatballs?" "Give me both at once," I would answer.

If there was still time I would go visit my third aunt, too. I never used to be a big eater, and my mother would run after me trying to get me to eat, but now all the time I was hungry. No matter how much I ate, I never had enough. My appetite was terrific. I was growing at that time and I needed more food. My only happiness was when my belly was bloated. When I had had enough I would start back home, well-filled and breathing heavily, like a goose. When I came in, Aunt Ettel would ask me, "Did you make the rounds already?"

"Yes."

"Did they give you something to eat?"

"Yes."

I would get ready for bed and in no time I would fall asleep. I would dream all kinds of dreams, and I would think that my uncle was waking me because I was yelling, but he was waking me because it was time to go to work. I felt so unwilling to go to work; I wished the Germans were as willing to fight as I was to go to work. If so, they wouldn't have started the war. I would have to pull my legs off the window sill. It didn't feel as if I had any legs left, and I would think I was paralyzed. Then I would start with the yawning and fall back to sleep until my uncle called, "Hershke, get up! You'll be late!" I had to jump up, wash myself in cold water, dress quickly, and say goodby as I ran out of the house. I was always the last one to arrive at the place where the people stood waiting to go to work. It looked like everyone had been waiting for me. As soon as I got in line, they would start marching out of the ghetto. I would be wishing we were on the way back. When I thought that I had to start a whole new day, I felt sad in my heart. I wasn't alone; everyone felt that way. We would walk with our heads hanging every morning.

12. The Big Liquidation

On the twenty-eighth of October 1941, ten thousand innocent people were taken from the ghetto to the Ninth Fort. It was a Tuesday. I was standing in line waiting to go to work. It got lighter and lighter, but our guards still did not come to pick us up. We were supposed to go out at six, but at eight they still hadn't arrived. Everyone started to get uneasy. All at once we looked around and could see that there were more guards at the fence. The German commander of all the guards came and told us in German that we should go back home. Today no one was going to work. As I walked home, I saw Uncle Abraham, who had been told to go home, too.

We felt right away that this was a day that would bring death. We started shaking with fear. The neighbors were all talking, trying to figure it out. Each would tell a new development, and the anxiety built. One would say, "Already some of the Gestapo have driven into the ghetto with Ukrainians and Lithuanians." It wasn't long until the soldiers began going into all the houses and dragging people out, telling them to run to the big brick building on Varniu Street. Right beside this building was an open field where there was a big hole. They used to bury all the rubbish there. It was so big it could have held twice the population of the ghetto.

As we were being rushed to the field, soldiers were stealing whatever they could. They would even take a coat off someone if they liked it. If they saw that you were wearing nice shoes, they would say, "Take them off. Where you are going, you won't need them anymore." Again, there was a little dais, and on it stood a tall, thin German high officer. When all the people were assembled, we were surrounded by Germans with machine guns pointing at us, waiting for the order to start shooting. Everyone was told to be quiet; the Gestapo leader was going to give a speech.

"We cannot afford to have any unproductive people in the ghetto. For the old and the sick we have a different place where they will be able to relax. They are only injuring the productive people. They take the rations from the working people. If we take them out, then the working people will be able to get more to eat."

What did it mean? People became panic-stricken as everyone started saying goodby to their dear ones. People prayed and women rung their hands and tore their hair from their heads. The screaming and crying could split the skies, but nobody answered our prayers or our tears. We let ourselves be led like sheep.

The Germans, Lithuanians, and Ukrainians ran between the lines of people, hitting them with their rifles; people fell like flies. This liquidation was carried out differently; they didn't want the Jewish police to go through first because they didn't want the other people to know which way was life. The same tragic scene began as people marched past the platform while the German pointed left or right. We didn't know which way was life and which was death.

This wasn't really a liquidation of the sick and old; it was just a way to kill so many people. The sick and old were an excuse, because in truth this massacre took away more young ones. The finger pointed one way or the other. The people who were sent in one direction would go to the other; some who were directed to the side of life ran to the side of death. Many were shot running from one side to the other. Some people went crazy; their minds couldn't take it. We could also see people dropping right to the ground, dead of heart attacks. My uncles and aunts were standing together and we decided that whatever our luck was, whichever way the finger pointed we would go. We would not run from one side to the other. Uncle Abraham, Aunt Ettel, and I were in front, and behind us were Uncle Yenchik and his family and Uncle Borach, Celia, and Maishke.

The Big Liquidation

As we came up to the dais in a group of about a hundred families, half of us were sent to one side and half to the other. We were in the half sent to the right and the other half was sent to the left. As we went past the dais, there weren't many people left to march by. The leader saw that it was getting dark, so he pushed people through faster. A half hour later, as our line marched past, we knew that whichever way the police went would be the good side. We saw that he sent the police to the right, and then we understood that we were on the side to live.

There started all kinds of cries and screams. Someone was screaming on the left side, "Don't leave me alone. Take me with you! Don't let me go!" Others were crying, "Save me! Don't let me die!" Young children were crying; all that screaming still rings in my ears.

Some cried, "Try at least to save my children, they are so young, their life is ahead of them!" But who could save them? Nobody could. This screaming didn't last long because all the people who were sent to the left were taken away to the little ghetto. Then the people on the right were told to get ready to go to work "voluntarily" for the night shift.

There were more volunteers than they needed. People thought that if they went to work they might be saved. After the volunteers were taken, the rest of the people went home. We were in shock, but when we got home and realized the situation, then the real tragedy began to sink in. One's husband, another's brother, another's children—everybody was missing someone from his family. After we learned that the people on the left had been taken to the little ghetto, we thought perhaps we would be able to see them again, that they were just being separated. No one knew what to think; everyone was dazed.

The most gruesome scene was played at two the next morning; the people were taken from the little ghetto to the Ninth Fort. I was on the night shift at the time, but the next morning when I came back home, my aunt and uncle took me in their arms and said, breaking into tears, that all the people had been taken to be shot. The whole ghetto was wrapped in a cloak of despair.

Even in this time of catastrophe there were a lot of Jews who said, "Somebody's bad luck is my good luck." Our Jewish brothers and sisters ran through the houses of those taken away and robbed them of food, clothing, whatever they could find. Later, when they went to work, they sold or traded the things for food or other items. In their eyes, the people were dead anyway.

In a word, there was a riot in the ghetto. Even the Jewish police, not being sure of themselves, let it run its course. Many people were afraid of their own Jewish neighbors' robbing and killing them, which is just what the Germans wanted.

The Jewish committee building was surrounded by thousands of Jews waiting for news from Dr. Elkes, who had gone to talk to Rauca. On the streets one heard, "Did you hear? Did Dr. Elkes come back yet? Is he back in the ghetto?" We waited for new orders. When he came back he gave an order to start printing what the Gestapo leader had told him to tell the survivors in the ghetto. The order read: "Jews, you shouldn't be afraid any more. From now on nothing will happen. We have taken the nonproductive people and that is in your favor, so you can have more to eat. From today on there should be enough people to go to work on all the brigades, because we need you to rebuild all the buildings and the airport and roads that the Russians destroyed when they retreated." It was signed by Dr. Elkes.

Some Jews listened to what they wanted to hear, that they would be safe from now on, and believed there would be no more executions. But there were many of us who didn't believe the murderers' new assurances. We had learned from all we had been through that any time the Germans said it was going to be good from now on, it would come out bad anyway. To be truthful, we knew we would all be killed, but we wanted to believe we would survive.

A couple of days later things returned to normal, with everyone going to work and things going according to schedule. The ghetto was thinned out; before the execution a lot of people would be on the street, but now the streets were empty. About 17,000 Jews were left, and each one knew that his luck was about used up. Everyone was looking for some way to save himself, to stay alive as long as he could.

13. The Workshops and the Small Brigades

The Germans decided that, as long as they were feeding the Jews, they might as well try to get the most work possible out of them, at least until the Jewish question was settled. This is why they started building a big factory in the ghetto with many different departments, including tailors, shoemakers, furriers, toymakers, and mechanics. When they were ready to begin production, it was up to the Jewish government leaders to supply workers for the jobs. They gave cards entitling people to work in the factory to their friends and relatives and to the friends and relatives of the Jewish police. When all of these people were taken care of, then other people could get the cards, if they could bribe a little. You also had to bribe the men who actually handed out the cards if you wanted one mailed directly to your house. Those who had handed in their valuables had nothing to bribe with, so they had to wait for a little luck.

The Germans wanted real shoemakers, furriers, and so forth, but many people who went to work at the factory had no skills, since they had been chosen just because of their connections. Every day long lines of people waited by the Jewish government building, even overnight, to get a card to work at the factory, sometimes only to find that all the positions were already filled. Fights broke out about who was ahead in the line. One would start pushing another, and a fight would continue until the Jewish police came and took the fighters to jail. The other people watching this would be very quiet, but as soon as the police were gone the fight would start again.

The distribution of work cards took a week. Uncle Abraham was lucky and got one. His trade had been tailoring, and he worked at this in the factory. About three thousand people worked in the workshops, and each was searched as he came and left work on either the day or the night shift. When my uncle came home from work, he would tell us that, of all the three thousand people working, only about five hundred were really skilled men; the rest were hiding under the coats of the skilled ones.

Everyone working in the workshops got an extra ration from the Germans, and also a very good extra ration of soup for lunch made of potatoes and beans. Uncle Abraham made new uniforms for the German soldiers by cleaning and repairing the uniforms of dead German soldiers. The shoe department made new boots and shoes for the soldiers. The furriers redesigned the furs the Jews had turned in for the wives of the German officers. The mechanical department cleaned and repaired machine-guns and handguns, and the toy department made toys that were sent to Germany for the German children. Every day big trucks would bring in the raw materials for this work and would take the new products back to Germany.

The main thing the Germans were proud of from this workshop was the toys because they had a tremendous effect on the German children. The toy workshop became so well known that every other day German high officers, even from Berlin, would come to look at the wonderful work of the Jewish workshops. Later on, as the toy department got even more famous, they made a special present for the big cannibal, Göring. It was a pipe for smoking. I myself didn't see the pipe, but I heard from people who did that it was so exquisite that even in the good days before the war you wouldn't have been able to find one like it. When the pipe was sent to Germany and didn't come back, it meant that the big Mr. Göring had accepted it, and there was joy in the whole ghetto. Maybe this would buy us some time.

The leader of the workshops was a man by the name of Mr. Segalson. He wasn't any relation to the police or the Jewish hierarchy, but he was a very good businessman. And since he was the leader of the workshops and became famous for the gift

The Workshops and the Small Brigades 71

of that pipe, all the Jewish police and the hierarchy became his people.

The Germans now started developing little work brigades. All the people who were working on the airfield tried to get into the smaller brigades. They didn't care what kind of work they got as long as they got away from the airfield, which was rough work. A lot of people who had worked in the small brigades would say, "Hey, I get plenty to eat and the Germans don't work us so hard." In the small brigades, you came into contact with the Lithuanians and if you had a gold watch or something, you could buy some butter or extra bread from them.

Mr. Goldberg, the man who handed out the working cards, also belonged to the Jewish Presidium. The little brigades followed the same pattern as the workshops. When the leaders heard what the good jobs were, they got their friends into those easier brigades, unless someone could bribe them. In this case you didn't need any gold; you could bribe by saying, "If you let me go to this brigade, I will bring you a couple of pounds of butter or pork or other food." Since all their friends were already in good positions, this kind of bargain worked.

At 5:00 AM we could already see lines of people standing beside the Jewish government headquarters, waiting to get a card. As before, everyone was yelling and fighting. Of five hundred people, maybe ninety of them would get cards. If you did get a card, it was only good for one month. After that, you had to try to renew it and promise to bring butter or something all over again. If you couldn't bribe, you would go no place. This was a very good deal for the Jewish hierarchy and the police. They didn't have to worry about food; people who went to work would bring them whatever they wanted—pork, butter, even liquor.

I stood in line to get a card for a little brigade, but my luck was to keep working on the airfield. Uncle Yenchik got a card to work in a Lithuanian hospital where there were many wounded German soldiers from the front line. His work was to unload the wounded and take them up to the hospital rooms. It was a hard job, but it had its revenge. He was a Jew carrying wounded soldiers; he could tell they weren't having it so good, either. He got plenty of food working there, as much as he wanted to eat, so much that he would bring some home. He would take an empty five-quart can to work and at night bring it home filled with soup. He would carry an empty sack and bring back good German rye bread. Besides this, he came in contact with Lithuanians, and they would sell food for valuables or money.

The same thing went on in the the other little brigades. With this extra food, the Jews started getting on their feet. As the little brigades became more numerous, the big ghetto became self-sufficient in food and drink. Little shops started opening where you could buy surplus food. You could buy anything, even liquor, but it took a lot of money. Who could afford it? The Jewish government officials, the Jewish police, and the people who had hidden all their valuables. The people who had no money or valubles couldn't buy any of this, but they weren't starving either—not the way it was in the ghettos in Warsaw and Lutz. In our ghetto there were some who, before the war, hadn't had it this good—people in the black market and the police. Now they were hoping the war would never be over.

14. The Jewish Police

There were two groups of police. One kept order in the ghetto and the second, the fence police, stood by the ghetto fence with the Germans and Lithuanians, waiting for the incoming Jewish working brigades to inspect what they brought in in their knapsacks, to see if there was anything not allowed. Earlier in the war, we were permitted to bring food into the ghetto—say, one pound of butter, one bottle of milk, one loaf of bread, and two pounds of potatoes—but sometimes there would be an order that nothing was to come in, and if the police found anything at all they would take it away.

Our ghetto had two gates through which people would come to work, one on Varniu Street and the second on Krisciukaicio Street. On the average, one man from every family was working in a small brigade. In the evening, around seven or eight, you could see women and children pushing buggies to the fence where the men would pass on their way home. We used to call them zippers. They would pull the buggies close to the fence. Nervously they would wait as the brigades came in. If the first brigade went through the police inspection without a fuss, it meant that they weren't taking anything away. Then the women would say in Yiddish, so that the men on the other side could hear, "Tonight we will be able to pull much food into the ghetto." But when they could see that the inspection dragged on and the police were seizing packages, the women would call, "Fire, fire! It's burning!" to warn the men.

Some men carried heavy knapsacks. As soon as they heard the screaming they knew the Germans and the police were taking everything away, so they would panic. Those with full knapsacks would push to the back, hoping that the guards would tire of the inspection and let the rest go through. Everyone wanted to be last. Many people ran into private Lithuanians' yards and hid themselves to wait, and others ran up to the fence and threw their knapsacks over to their families, who would catch them and put them in the buggies. Then the Germans and Lithuanians would start shooting in the air to create a panic. Other people took a risk and whispered to the guards that they would bribe them to go through the fence. Sometimes the guard would cut the fence and hold it while the Jew put the sack through and crawled after, but it didn't always work. Sometimes the guard would take whatever he was given and then take the man to the German commander. What was done then, I don't have to tell you.

When the Jewish police saw a friend or relative, they would pull him through the gate. The Germans didn't pay any attention to what the Jewish police were doing. On a day when it wasn't good to go through the gate, you could see piled by the fence a lot of knapsacks filled with food. When all the brigades had gone through, the Jewish police would bring up a wagon and load all the knapsacks to take away to the police bureau, where they divided the food among themselves.

I heard later that some of those in the Jewish police were involved in the resistance movement and helped the council shield others who were wanted by the Gestapo. This may be true. We didn't know any of this at the time. All we knew was that we didn't want anything to do with members of the police or even of the Jewish Presidium. To meet up with one of them could only mean trouble. We suffered from the blows and kicks of the police and being dragged out of our homes into one working brigade or another, not knowing if we would return. This is why we felt so bitter as we watched the Jewish police living well while we did the backbreaking labor and went begging for food. We saw them working hand in hand with the Germans. What the Germans said the police would carry out to the letter. The time would come when they would suffer like all the others, but that is a chapter for later.

15. New Life and New Work

After the massacre my whole family and I saw that there was no hope of crawling out of the lion's claws. It was only a matter of time. The moment would arrive when the bloodthirsty animal would tear us apart as it had torn apart ten thousand other Jews. We had no choice but to wait for death. We had no valuables, even if we could have found a trustworthy Lithuanian to hide us. We had come naked from the little ghetto and often went to bed hungry, so how could we think of saving ourselves? We had to tear the empty illusions from our heads.

One nice morning I went out to work at the airport. I was standing in line waiting for the guards to come pick us up when two Jewish police ran up to the line and stood me to one side, saying, "Don't go anyplace; stay right here." Who knew for what or where they would take me? Before long they pulled out seven other boys my age and put us in two lines of four each. They took us through the gate to a German guard. The guard looked us over and told us to follow him.

We passed by the Slobodka bridge and turned onto the main street. On the corner of Duonelaicio we came to a stop in front of a large hotel. The German took us into the kitchen through the back entrance. He told the chef that he had brought eight Jews, and the chef came up to stare at us. Our eyes and noses, however, were drawn toward the food. The aroma was tearing my nose apart. The big German officers stayed in this hotel. The chef told us that we would have to drive sixty miles to load some potatoes and bring them back to the kitchen and that a Lithuanian would come with a truck to drive us there. "In the meantime," he said,

"I will give you something to eat." Can you imagine our feelings as we heard the word "food"? Our mouths started watering. Soon we were sitting down at the table in the kitchen. The first course was a big plate of German potato salad with little pieces of meat in it. In the blink of an eye that plate was cleared. It was not just empty; the dishwasher didn't even have to wash it! The second thing we got was a soup thick with meat and fresh little carrots. It tasted like manna from heaven. After this came dessert: pudding with marmalade on top. When we finished dessert, we were feeling hungry instead of starved. Nobody moved from the table.

The chef looked at us and saw what was going on, so he said, "If you want more to eat, you can get more." Everybody got up with his plate and the real meal started. One after another would come and go with his plate. I didn't count how many servings the others had, but I know that I had six bowls of soup. Everyone in the kitchen stared at us, wondering where we put it all. When our stomachs were full we moved from the table into the yard where the Lithuanian driver was waiting for us. He told us to crawl into the back of the truck for the ride to the little town of Ariogala. No other guard went with us. The truck was open and as we rode the wind cut through our clothes and chilled us to the bone. It took three hours, and all that time we talked only about the food we had eaten at the hotel.

At the field where we were supposed to load the potatoes were many Lithuanian farmers with carts full of potatoes they had to give up to the Germans without pay. The Lithuanians looked at us with our yellow stars and gathered around us, crossing themselves. They told us they had thought there were no Jews left alive. One farmer took out a big loaf of dark bread and gave it to me. Another farmer gave me a large piece of cured pork. They gave us whatever they had. It was a different world. When the Lithuanian who had brought us saw that we were taking too long to load the potatoes, he yelled to the farmers to get away and told us to start loading. While we filled the truck, the driver went to warm himself in a little bar by the road.

We started talking to the farmers again. "Where are all the Jews from this town?"

"They were all shot the first day the Germans came in."

I asked one farmer, "If I come here tomorrow, may I bring some things to sell so I can buy food?"

"Sure," he said, and at the same time he gave me a live chicken and a sack for potatoes. I cut off the head of the chicken.

We sat on top of the potatoes and waited for the driver. He didn't come out, so we went to the bar to see what was happening. When we saw the driver sitting on a chair drinking from a bottle of whiskey, we understood what we had to do. If we came back tomorrow, we had to get some money so we could buy him whiskey and let him get drunk. While he was drinking we could do business with the farmers.

When he saw us, he got up from his chair and told us to go back to the truck for the trip home. On the way back, we filled our sacks, our pockets, anything we could, with potatoes. We wondered how we could get through the gate with all this food. When we got close to the fence, the Lithuanian stopped the truck. We told him that he should drive to the gate and report that he was returning eight Jews from a hard day's work. He listened to us and drove right up to the gate on Varniu street and told the guards what we had told him to say. It was dark, about 8:00 PM, and the two Lithuanian guards opened the gate and we got in without being searched. After we passed through the gate we stopped. Two young men from our group jumped down and the other six started handing down our sacks of potatoes. The Lithuanian driver helped us. When we were unloaded the Lithuanian told us that we should wait for him the next morning in a separate line and that he would come pick us up to go to work. We were excited about this. After he left with the truck, we got together and decided where we would meet the next morning.

As I walked home, the weight of the potatoes made me puff like a locomotive and I was wringing wet with sweat. But I couldn't wait to show my aunt and uncle all the things I had. It took me over an hour to reach home. When Aunt Ettel and Uncle Abraham saw me with the big sack and bulging pockets they couldn't understand what it was all about. First I threw down the bag from my shoulder. I took off my coat and started emptying all the potatoes from my pockets. Then I sat down and told my story. I asked my uncle to find something for me to trade for food the next day, so he went to some friends to borrow money and a few pieces of clothing. I started washing up and Aunt Ettel began unpacking the potatoes. She put her hand in the bag and pulled out the headless chicken. Her first question was, "Hershke, who cut off its head?"

I said, "The Lithuanian," because I had never done anything like that and I wasn't sure that she would approve.

When Uncle Abraham came home he sat down to have supper. He had gotten fifty German marks and three women's blouses. We sat down to eat, and Aunt Ettel told him what she had found in the sack. He started laughing; it was like a big holiday. This supper was the best my aunt had ever prepared, but she didn't cook the chicken.

"The chicken," she said, "we are going to have for the Sabbath. We are also going to invite Aunt Golda and Aunt Celia and their families.

It would be just like the good days before the Germans.

When I finished eating I got ready for bed. Before turning out the light, I told my uncle to remember to come wait for me the next night by the fence and to bring a buggy if he could borrow one.

The next morning we eight young men stood together and waited to go through the gate. We heard someone yell, "The potato brigade! Potato brigade through the gate." The Lithuanian was there waiting for us. We went back to the hotel and unloaded the potatoes from the day before into the cellar. The cook fed us again. We finished eating and went back for another load. As we rode, we kept asking each other, "Did you remember to bring something to trade?" Each of us took out twenty marks and put it together to take care of the driver. We decided between us that as soon as we got to the town we would start loading the potatoes so that it wouldn't take long. In the meantime I would go to the bar with the Lithuanian and get him a bottle of whiskey and a sandwich.

As soon as we arrived we jumped from the truck and started loading as fast as we could. When the driver decided that he didn't have to watch us he went to the bar. I left the rest of the boys loading and ran after him.

He asked me, "What are you doing here?"

I told him in a low voice, "I am going to warm up a little."

"The only way to warm up is to have a little whiskey," he answered.

I said nothing but went up to the barmaid and asked her to sell me a bottle of whiskey and a big piece of sausage. She gave me that and a large loaf of bread. I took it all over to the Lithuanian and told him, "Hey, drink. Have a good time." He didn't ask any questions but started gulping right from the bottle. As he neared the end of the bottle, he remembered me and said, "Do you want a drink?"

"No," I said, "I don't drink."

He finished the bottle and started eating. I could tell that he was feeling pretty warmed already, so I brought him another bottle, put on my coat, and went back to my friends.

They ran up and asked, "How did it work?"

"Everything is okay and it cost me just eighty marks." We divided the eighty marks left over among us. The truck was loaded so we each took an empty bag and went to a different farmhouse.

I came to a farmhouse where the whole family was sitting by a covered table eating. When they saw me the father asked what I wanted. I told him that I was a Jew and I had some nice things that I wanted to trade. Everyone sitting at the table heard me say that I was a Jew and they jumped up, startled.

"The first thing we are going to do," the farmer said, "is eat. After we finish eating then we will talk business." They gave me a chair at the head of the table and brought out a big gefilte fish and gave me a large glass of whiskey. We made our toast in Lithuanian and started eating. Before long the farmer offered me another glass of whiskey and I drank it. His wife brought in a big roast with browned potatoes. With such a nice piece of meat, of course, we had to have another glass of whiskey. By the time I was done eating I had to loosen my belt.

After dinner we talked of business and I took out the three blouses and showed them to the wife. As I started my sales pitch,

I told her that it was the best merchandise you could find. I held a blouse up near her face so she could see how it looked against her skin. She took all three and went to try them on to see if they fit. She asked her husband how she looked, and he, having had quite a few glasses of whiskey, mumbled through his nose, "It fits perfectly." Luckily, all the blouses were her size. She took them and asked about the price.

I answered that I wanted food. I told her that for all three blouses she should give me two pounds of butter, one goose, two pounds of pork, five pounds of flour, two chickens, a loaf of bread, three dozen eggs, and two quarts of milk. In truth, I didn't know what to ask.

"That is too much," she said.

"If that is too much, what is enough?" I asked. "I tell you what, let's ask your husband."

He was sitting with his head on the table, snoring. She woke him and he said, half asleep, "Give him everything he wants."

His wife took my knapsack and went to put everything in it. I went with her to help, but my legs were shaky after all that whiskey, and my head started spinning. I managed not to lose my balance, however, and I saw that everything was put in the sack. When we were finished I went back to say goodby to the farmer. He got up and told his wife to bring more food and whiskey.

"I can't drink any more," I told him. "I won't be able to walk back and you'll have to take me."

"If you don't drink with me," he answered, "I'll give you all the blouses back and take back all my goods."

I had no choice. I held my breath and swallowed the glass of whiskey, took my knapsack on my back, said goodby, and ran out of the house. I felt my head spinning in all directions. I saw double. I had a long way to go to meet my friends and the Lithuanian, but I didn't give up; I walked, wobbling, and kept checking to make sure that I still had my sack on my shoulders.

When I came to the place where the truck should have been waiting with the loaded potatoes, I saw no truck, no people. I was afraid and looked around frantically with my bleary eyes. I ran into the little bar and asked where the Lithuanian driver was.

New Life and New Work

The woman told me that my group had left a long time ago. When I heard those words, I sobered up quickly. I walked out of the bar not knowing what to do. If they were coming back the next day, I could sleep in the field. I crawled into the big hole where the potatoes were and used my knapsack for a pillow, putting my coat under my back.

I fell asleep only to be awakened with a start by a siren. I looked up and, not far from me, saw two big trucks. On the trucks were six people wearing yellow stars. I ran up to them and looked at them because I didn't believe they were Jews. I asked them in Yiddish where they came from. They asked me if I were Jewish too and I told them my story. They told me not to worry, that they were going to load up both trucks and go back to the ghetto. I could go with them.

The truck drivers who came with these people were Germans. One driver tried to back his truck up to the area where the potatoes were, but he got his rear wheels stuck in a sandy area. We tried to push it forward and backward but it wouldn't budge. The Lithuanian farmers were called on to help, but without success. It began to rain, falling harder and harder until one driver said that we would get into the other truck and drive into town to look for something to eat and a place to sleep.

I took my knapsack and got in with the rest of the Jews in the back of the second truck and rode into town. We stopped by a little house, and one man from our brigade ran in to ask the owner to make us something to eat. He agreed and we all went in.

Soaked from the rain, we sat around the big table, and again I saw lots of food and whiskey. The farmer's wife brought out a big plate of boiled ham and potatoes. I took only a few bites, but the rest of the Jews and the German drivers ate and drank a great deal. We sat eating and drinking from eight in the evening until midnight.

At that time one driver said to the other, "Go see what's happening outside. Maybe the rain has stopped and we can go back and try to get the truck out." Some of the Jews went outside and came back saying that it had stopped raining and was now a fine night.

The second driver said, "All you Jews, we're going to take you to the town jail to sleep."

The first said, "No, we'll go back and start loading the potatoes." Both argued, pretty drunk, and finally decided we would go load potatoes. We said goodby to the Lithuanians. The Jews paid for their food, but from me they would take nothing. I took my sack again and climbed into the truck.

As soon as we got back to the truck, we tried again to get the other truck out of the mud but still couldn't do it. We loaded the one truck and decided to sleep in the field and drive back in the morning. I put my sack on the top of the loaded potatoes and went to sleep.

When I awoke, the others were still asleep. I got up and began stretching. Then I looked up and saw that the truck loaded with potatoes wasn't there. I woke the others, but no one knew what had happened. The German driver awoke and told us that the other driver had gotten up at 3:00 AM and driven home.

I realized then that all my work had gone to the devil. I didn't know what to do. It got lighter and the farmers came with their potatoes. With the help of the farmers with their teams of horses we finally got the truck out of the mud. We loaded the potatoes and started home.

As we sat on the potatoes, I saw my companions from yesterday coming back with the empty truck to load more potatoes. I decided to go back with the truck I was on, since my sack had gone ahead already and I wanted to find it if I could.

While we were driving I thought about my knapsack loaded with food and wondered how I could find it. I wasn't interested in the stories of the others, I just kept thinking about my lost sack. As we drove along we saw on the right-hand side of the road a truck sitting loaded with potatoes. The truck that had left early had had a flat tire! When I saw my sack on top of the potatoes I felt ecstatic. I jumped off the truck, got the sack, and put it on my shoulder.

We helped the driver. It took us four or five hours to fix the flat. We drove into town and unloaded the potatoes. By that time it was seven in the evening. I thought we would go back to the ghetto, but the rest of the Jews said they would sleep there and

New Life and New Work

go back for more potatoes the next day. I told them that I was going back to the ghetto since my aunts and uncles would be wondering what had happened to me.

I thought about how to get back. I was not far from the Gestapo headquarters; if they found me I would be dead. I put all the potatoes I could into the sack and took off my stars. I mixed with the Lithuanians and started toward the ghetto. My heart was pounding and I kept looking left and right, watching for someone who might stop me. When I saw the Slobodka bridge, I thought that I would cross it and hide myself by a doorway until some brigade came by; I would mix in with that brigade to get through the gate. While I waited in hiding, each minute seemed like a year. Finally I saw a brigade of about thirty Jews coming and jumped in, asking the man behind me to put on my yellow stars. Now I belonged to that brigade.

My next problem was getting through the gate without being inspected. I was praying the German Gestapo commandant would not be by the gate. If he wasn't there, everything would be okay. As we got closer to the gate we were thrown under a big searchlight. I saw the green coat of the commandant; it looked bad. I dropped back in the line and took out of my pocket five marks to have in my hand for whoever inspected me. I wanted to be sure I was inspected by a Lithuanian.

When we came to the gate the guard told the commander that he was bringing thirty Jews from a cleaning brigade. The commandant looked over the Jews with filled bags, pulling one and another from the line. When he pulled one out, I seized the moment and ran up to the Lithuanian inspecting the Jews. He pushed on my pockets and felt my bag. As he reached toward my right pocket I put the five marks in his hand. He understood what I meant and stopped searching, but he took a bottle of milk I had in my coat as he told me to go. I was bothered by the fact that he had taken the milk; on the other hand I knew that he could have taken everything. I hoped he would drink the milk and it would kill him. The main thing was that I would be home soon and able to tell my aunt and uncle what had happened and show them what I had bought for the three blouses. I started walking faster and was soon home.

I opened the door slowly. Inside I could hear many people; the voices were familiar. I took off the sack and left it by the door before I walked in. The first one to see me was Aunt Ettel. She ran up and put her arms around me. She had tears in her eyes and said, "Here's Hershula!" I didn't know what to say. "You went out of the house to work healthy and happy and you didn't come back."

I answered, "But here I am and what happened to me was I lost my friends when I went to work." Uncle Abraham came in and cried out, "Look who is here, Hershula, Hershke is here!" I looked around and there were Aunt Golda with her family, Uncle Borach and Aunt Celia and Maishke. I didn't understand what was going on with this scene from out of the past.

Aunt Ettel, with tears still in her eyes, told me, "Today is the Sabbath." I had forgotten about the chicken and the Sabbath.

"I don't know," I said, "but if they came to eat chicken, let's eat chicken!"

Everyone was happy to see me alive and healthy. As we started to sit at the table, I took the bag with the potatoes and food to Aunt Ettel, telling her to unpack carefully since there were some breakable things inside. She was excited to see what I had brought, so she let her guests wait for a while and started unpacking with my help. The first thing she pulled out was the goose. Astonished, she called out, "Abraham! Come look what Hershke brought us."

He ran in with my other aunts and uncles. Aunt Ettel held the goose up by the legs. Everyone asked where I had gotten it.

I answered, "I am gone away from home a day and a night, you think I am going to bring nothing? Not just the goose. I brought some better things that we can have on another Sabbath. Next Saturday you will be able to come and eat cake."

My aunt was so involved in unpacking that she forgot we were all ready to eat the chicken. All the good food was on the table and you could see that everyone's mouth was watering. When I saw everyone looking at these things, I said to my aunt, "What's happening to the chicken? Is it cooked? I'm hungry. Let's go and eat."

Aunt Ettel ran to the stove and took the chicken out, cutting it into ten portions. Every portion was a good size, since it was a large chicken. As we ate everybody asked me questions.

"Hershke, where have you been? How did you get that? How did you get through the gate with all that stuff?" Everyone was curious. I told them the whole story from beginning to end. Everyone listened with open mouths.

When I finished, my uncles and aunts and cousins began getting ready to leave. I was so tired that I rested my head on the table, hearing them talk in whispers, saying goodby. I lifted my head to say goodby and asked them to remember to come back next Saturday for goose and cake. I was drifting away to sleep just like in the old days, before the war, when my mother and father used to take me into the bedroom I shared with Uncle Schloime and I would fall asleep listening to their guests talking and saying goodby.

Then I heard my aunts say, "With God's help, we will be healthy and there will be no more purges. We won't have to be reminded; we'll be here."

As I was getting ready for bed after they left, Aunt Ettel came up to me and said that she had a nice present for me. She took out a little cardboard box and opened it. Inside was a brand new shirt. She told me that she had traded some potatoes for it. I tried it on and it fit perfectly. I thanked her and told her that I could keep my eyes open no longer, I was so tired. I fell asleep immediately.

Suddenly Uncle Abraham was calling me to go to work. I thought I was dreaming, but it was morning and it was no dream. I went to the place where I was supposed to meet my friends and went back with them to work. I decided that this time I would not go too far from the truck to deal with the farmers because I didn't want to repeat what had happened before. I decided to deal with the farmers who brought potatoes to the field.

Every day I brought food back to the ghetto. Because of that food we became better off and began to trade food for clothing and other things we needed. We began to get on our feet. We had enough to eat and I no longer went to bed hungry. It didn't last long.

When the Jewish police detected that our potato brigade was a good place to work and that we were coming back with big sacks of food, they began looking at us to see if we had any connections with the police or Jewish government. Since I had no connections, they took me off the brigade and sent me back to work at the airfield, putting one of their friends in my place. I had worked in that brigade for two weeks.

It had been like heaven in the potato brigade and now the airfield brigade seemed like hell. I was no longer used to the hard work and walking again day in and day out to the airport, and now I couldn't bring anything home.

One day as I came home I noticed that my right leg was hurting but I thought it would go away. When I tried to get up the next morning, however, I couldn't stand on the leg, it was so swollen. I couldn't go to work but I wasn't allowed to stay home, so I didn't know what to do. The Jewish police might come search the house for people not working. If they found me they would take me to jail. I decided that what would be would be. I couldn't put on my shoe so I couldn't go to work. If things were quiet, I would try to get to the ghetto doctor.

The doctor had the power to give me a furlough so that I would be excused from work until my leg got better. As it neared lunchtime my leg was worse. I put on my shoe and put my right leg into a rubber boot. I started dragging myself to the doctor, Nachimovski. This doctor was a bandit! He gave no one furloughs unless they had connections or could bribe him. A furlough cost two pounds of butter or a bottle of schnapps. If you could pay, you didn't even have to show up in his office, he would mail the furlough to you. I had no temperature so I was sure he wouldn't give me a furlough.

When I got to the office I was the second in line. The first patient left and I went in. Sitting behind the desk was a little man with a big belly and fat cheeks. He asked me in a German Jewish accent what I wanted. I told him I hadn't gone to work today because I had pain in my leg and it was swollen and that I wanted a furlough. He told me to sit on the couch and take off my boot. He asked me how long I had had the pain.

He said nothing more but wrote out a furlough for three days.

New Life and New Work

You can understand how bad my leg looked for him to give me that furlough. I went home and told my aunt that I had gotten the furlough. She couldn't believe it.

My leg worsened. Our reserve of potatoes and other food from my work in the potato brigade was gone and we had started eating horse meat again. We thanked God for even that. Suddenly after eating supper one night Aunt Ettel got severe pains in her stomach. Day by day the pains grew worse. She went to the doctor but he told her it would go away. Then one day she couldn't even walk to the doctor so we had to get him to come to the house. He examined her and found that it was acute appendicitis. It was too late to do anything; it had already burst.

The only thing he could do was operate immediately. If he succeeded, she would become an invalid. He figured that her chances were one in a thousand. Uncle Abraham started running around like crazy. I was still in pain with my leg, and after three days got another furlough, but my leg kept getting worse.

Throughout all this trouble, we heard rumors that the Germans and Lithuanians were taking people into work brigades far past Kovno, but that I shouldn't worry because I had a furlough. Mostly I was frightened for my aunt. I could see how much she was suffering. She would lie in bed and scream from the pain.

Every evening, my uncles and aunts came to find out what was happening to Aunt Ettel, who had been taken to the hospital. We visited her and stood by her bed. She told us that as long as we were with her the pains were quiet. In truth she was on her deathbed but she didn't know it. We begged the doctor not to tell her what kind of sickness she had.

16. Koshedar

It was October 1942. My second furlough ended on Tuesday night; I planned to go get an extension on Wednesday morning, but Wednesday morning turned out to be too late. At five in the morning two Jewish policemen came to the door with an order in hand for Hershke Gordon.

I said, "I am Hershke Gordon."

"Get dressed and come with us."

"Where am I going? Already for about a week I haven't been able to go to work and my leg is still swollen."

One policeman answered, "We can do nothing. You had to extend the furlough yesterday. As long as you didn't, you have to go with us now. You will have enough time, as long as you need. We are taking you to the jail and the Jewish doctor will examine you there. If he says you cannot work, he will tell you to come back home."

Uncle Abraham and Aunt Ettel, who had been brought back from the hospital, were both awake. Uncle Abraham, who had been listening to our talk, jumped up from the couch and with a nervous voice started yelling, "What do you want from us? Aren't we already punished enough by God? Isn't that enough? Now you come adding even more suffering. My wife is lying on her deathbed; the boy is in bed with a swollen leg, swollen as big as a hill, and now you want to take him away? He can't even get dressed! He cannot wear shoes! It is hard for him to even walk."

The police didn't answer him. They told me again to get dressed. One policeman told the other to stay with me until I was dressed while he looked up the other people. I started getting dressed, but when I took my leg from the bed to put on my shoe, it wouldn't go on. I was in such pain that I broke into a sweat.

The policeman looked at me and my leg, which was swollen to twice the normal size, and told me to put on a rubber boot instead. I found a boot and put it on, holding onto my uncle as I did. I went into the room where my aunt was in bed. She saw as I came into the room that I was leaning against the wall, I was in such pain.

She, too, was in great pain and upset by my situation. She began to cry and to ask the policeman, "Don't take him away from me. I feel that these are my last few days. At least you could let him stay here and be here for my funeral. I treated him as good as his own mother." He answered, "If it was my mother's funeral, it couldn't be."

What happened then I will never forget as long as I live. The policeman started to cry. He had seen my pain as I got dressed and he felt my aunt's pain at my leaving; now he was crying bitter tears.

My aunt calmed down a little, and the policeman said to me, "You wait here. I will go myself to Dr. Goldberg and see if I can get the furlough. Don't go anywhere or try to hide; just wait here until I get back."

He left and I sat on my aunt's bed. My uncle was pacing back and forth nervously, saying nothing. The silence lasted for an hour. At eight in the morning the policeman came in with his head hanging and told me that the doctor would not give me any furlough.

"I have to go like this," I asked, "with one shoe and one boot? Where are we going? Should I take some clothes or something with me?"

"Don't take anything. The doctor down there will give you a furlough and send you back home."

Aunt Ettel began to cry again and now I would go through the worst. I had to say goodby to my aunt and uncle. I went up to Uncle Abraham, hugged and kissed him and told him, "Be well. Be healthy. Good day." His eyes were filled with tears, but he was trying to hold them back for the sake of Aunt Ettel. My heart was heavy as I walked up to her bed and hugged her. She wouldn't let me go. She pulled me to her, squeezing me stronger and stronger.

She cried and said to me, "Hershula, don't go away from me. Just let me hug you and kiss you, because this is the last I am going to see you. I am not going to see you again."

I couldn't hold out any more. I let out a hysterical cry, "Aunt Ettel, I am not going away from you. I am going to be with you, but only in my mind." When I finished saying goodby to my aunt, the policeman told me that we had to go.

I walked along the street trying to hold onto something with my right hand becase of the pain in my leg. I clung to the walls as I walked and I couldn't wait to reach the ghetto jail.

At the police office the policeman told them the whole story of what had happened and why I walked the way I did. There were two men in the office. One was tall and thin with long hands and glasses hanging on the edge of his nose; he was the secretary for the office. The second Jewish man was very short and had gray hair and long hanging cheeks. His name was Zaks. He was the working inspector.

After listening to the policeman's story, Zaks said, "Later on a doctor is going to come in and make sure everybody is healthy. If he finds anyone sick, he is going to send them back home. In the meantime, you will have to stay in the ghetto jail." He called up another policeman to take me into the jail.

There were a lot of other people waiting in the jail. Some were resting on bunk beds and many sat on benches. There were young girls and boys, married couples, and even families with little babies. Everyone had a sack of belongings; some had pillows, some clothes. They all yelled at the policeman and called him names. Everyone looked at me as if they felt sorry for me and each asked me how I came to be there with one shoe and one boot, with no clothes or provisions. I told them my story and that the policeman told me that a doctor would come and let the sick ones go back home. They laughed at me.

"Ha! That doctor will come here and let you go back home? They were lying to you! There will come no doctors. It's a joke. Doctors, shmoctors! Listen, you have a little time yet; why don't you see if you can get a few clothes or a pillow? If you are here, you are going where we are going."

"Where are they taking us?" I asked.

The man I was talking to answered, "I have a policeman friend and he told me they are taking us to a working camp to dig peat. The camp is called Koshedar (Kaisiadorys)."

I didn't want to believe it because the policeman who had brought me to the jail had gone to the doctor to get me taken off the list. He had told me the doctor would come to examine the sick, so I believed him. Besides, how was I going to work? I was on only one leg. Every little while I would hobble up to the window of the jail and ask the guard if the doctor had arrived. His answer was always, "No." It was 10:00 AM and the doctor was still not there. I lost all hope of getting out.

Then trucks with Germans who had come to pick us up began arriving in the jail yard. I sat in a corner and starting crying. I had no clothes, no shirt, nothing. All I had was a bad leg. Before long the door opened and a policeman came in and said, "Everybody get ready to move into the trucks."

I saw that I could say nothing to anyone, so I decided to go up to the German officer who had come to pick us up and show him my leg and ask him how I could work with such a leg. A couple of policemen came into the jail and told us to stand in a line. They took us out into the yard where there were German Wehrmacht. These were the people we would work for. I saw that the Germans called one man the *Hauptmann,* the man who delegated work to others. He was standing there talking to the Jewish column leader. Every working brigade had a column leader appointed by the Jewish authorities. He wore a white band on his arm and did not have to work; he just had to make sure that the rest of the Jews worked.

I stepped out of my line, limping, went up to the German *Hauptmann,* and said in German, "I have a bad leg and I can't work."

He told me to take off my boot and sock and show him my leg. Quickly I did so and he went to the police captain. He told the captain to bring a replacement for me since I would not be able to work, but the captain told him that there were no other people there.

The column leader came up to me and said, "Don't worry. You won't have to work. If your leg doesn't get better, we'll send you back to the ghetto. In the meantime, you'll have to come with us."

I saw that there was nothing I could do, so I asked them to allow me to go get some clothes, but it was too late. The *Hauptmann* ordered us to get into the trucks. There were ten trucks; into each truck went twenty people and their belongings. We sat in the trucks and waited for the order to move.

My heart ached as I sat there. Before my eyes was the picture of leaving home, leaving my sick aunt and my uncle. I had the feeling that I would never see my aunt again. I felt only despair. I thought I would have been lucky if the Germans had shot me right there and then and I could forget my troubles. How long could I suffer? My head pounded like a hammer.

When I heard the order to drive away I jumped as if I had been asleep. The motors started and the ghetto began to fall behind us until it disappeared from sight. I thought I would never see my family again and began to imagine all sorts of bad things that might happen.

The others in the truck saw how depressed I was; they talked to me, trying to lift my spirits. But I didn't answer them. I was deep in my thoughts, hoping for a miracle. My heart and soul were in the ghetto with my aunt.

We drove for five or six hours until we came to the little town of Koshedar. Two miles past the town our truck stopped in a field where our new camp would be. There were two barracks, both unfinished, without windows or doors. We had to finish building our new home. When I heard the order to get off the truck I woke as from a bad dream. We stood in a line and were counted to make sure no one was missing. They put one hundred people in each barracks.

I thought I would be able to lie down on a bunk bed and rest, but there were no bunk beds. Everyone had to sleep on the ground. At least some people had covers or pillows; all I had under me was my back. And soon we heard a call to come outside and line up again.

We were taken to a nearby German camp where we got two blankets and a quart of soup with a two-pound loaf of bread for every three people. Eating the bread and soup, I began to feel a little less sad. I thought the food and blankets were miracles, really.

The next morning we were awakened by a big *Lagerfuhrer* calling for everyone to line up outside and be ready to go to work. It didn't take me long to get ready, since I had slept in my clothes. I was the first to leave the barracks and go out to the field. The German *Hauptmann* was there with six Ukrainian volunteers. He started choosing people to work on the barracks. He left fifty to work in camp, told the children to go back to the barracks, and sent the rest to dig in the peat fields. I was left with the barracks brigade.

My job was to pick up little boards and give them to a couple of carpenters. The people who worked in the peat fields were each assigned a piece of land fifteen yards long and ten yards wide and were told to dig the peat three feet deep. They stood up to their knees in water and had to finish this piece of land on the first day. When they returned, dead tired, we had to stand in line to be counted before we were taken to the kitchen to get our ration of bread and soup.

We were given a thick soup made with potatoes and beans and went back to the barracks to finish our meal. As we sat eating, the door opened and in came the six Ukrainian guards. One had a guitar, another had a balalaika, a third had a harmonica, and the fourth an accordian, the fifth had two spoons, and the sixth nothing. They sat with us on the floor and started singing Russian gypsy music. After that they sang Russian folk songs and began dancing. The whole barracks began to hum and you could feel the vibration as they started singing and dancing and playing. Even though we felt bad, a faint flicker of life stirred among us. We began singing and dancing with them. Everyone forgot their troubles.

At ten in the evening they quieted down and started telling us how they came to join the German army. The Germans took them prisoner. Knowing they could not last long as prisoners, they volunteered to join the army, but they did not plan to stay in the army long. There were some very dense forests nearby where there were many guerrilla fighters. Once in a while they met with them. When the time was right, they would close ranks with the guerrillas. That is what happened, but not while I was in the camp. When the rest of the people were brought back to the ghetto they told me that the six Ukrainian guards had gone away to join the guerrillas in the woods.

The next morning, we went back to the same jobs, but the people digging in the fields were given even larger plots of land to dig. Those who worked fast came back early, but over half the camp had to stay late, many until midnight, working by kerosene lantern. When they came back, they were so tired they did not get their rations, but just fell into bed. So it went, day in and day out.

I saw that my leg was getting worse rather than better. How my aunt was doing, I didn't know. I was in such a state of worry, I didn't know what to do. In the middle of the day on the first Sunday we were in camp, the column leader and the German camp leader came to tell us that a team of German doctors was coming to camp and that whoever was sick would be able to go in for a checkup. If he was really sick, he would be excused from work.

Right away rumors spread that this would not be a doctor team but a death team. Nobody should go, because if they found out that you were sick they would not play around with you; they would kill you, or, as the Jewish expression went, "You would be gone from the market." Everyone was scared. They thought there would be a new massacre.

I thought, "I have nothing to lose. What is going to happen will happen. My life is lost anyway. I am going to go and tell them about my leg."

At four in the afternoon the leader of the German camp came and yelled in German, "All who are sick come outside." You could hear nothing in the barracks. No one moved. I got up and limped onto the field. I was the only one. The German took me into a room where five Germans were sitting; they looked like they were doctors. On one table there were a lot of empty whiskey bottles, and I could smell the liquor.

"Is this the only one who is sick?" they asked. They asked me in German, "What hurts?"

"My leg."

They told me to sit on a chair. I took off my boot and sock, and they started fiddling around with my leg. They asked me how long I had had the problem and talked between themselves in German. They handled me very nicely. They also asked the German leader what kind of work I had been doing. They did not tell me to put on my boot and sock.

They conferred in German, and since I understood German, I listened. At the end, the oldest of them, a lieutenant, got up and looked the German leader right in the eye and said, "From tomorrow on, he should do nothing. He should sit in the sun and let his leg bake in the heat."

The leader saluted and said, "I will see to it that he does what he is told."

After this I went back to the barracks. Everyone clustered around me and asked what happened. I told them, but no one would believe me. Everyone thought that I was joking.

"You can laugh now," I said, "but tomorrow morning you will see. While all of you work in the peat fields I will be out getting a suntan."

The next morning, when everyone was ready to go to work, the German leader came up to me and told me to leave the line. I walked to the side and waited. When everyone else left for work, he came up with the camp leader and told me to come with them. They took me to a place where boards were stacked up and the sun was shining as hot as fire. The leader told me to take off my boot and sock and put my leg in the sun. He stood there until I did so and then walked away. After he left, I began making myself comfortable. I was still afraid he was watching. I could hardly believe this was happening. I took off my coat and shirt, put them under my head and spread myself out. It was so hot that soon I was covered with sweat. An hour later the camp leader came up and asked me how I felt. I told him I felt good, and he walked away. I stayed there until the sun went down. As I walked back to the barracks I felt that my leg was a lot lighter than it had been in the morning. The swelling had gone down a little. The other people saw that I had really been lying in the sun, and they were jealous. One told another, "Look, I am sick too. I didn't go the the doctor. You shouldn't believe what others tell you. If I had gone, they would have freed me from work too and I would have been able to lie in the sun the whole day."

I could feel every day that my leg was getting better. At the end of the second week, the column leader came up to me as I was resting in the sun and said that he had good news for me.

"What kind?" I asked.

"Come with me and I will tell you," he said.

I got up in a hurry and ran back to the barracks, getting more and more anxious for the news. When I was in the barracks, he told me, "Gordon, I got a letter from the ghetto, from the Jewish Presidium, that you should come back to the ghetto."

I didn't believe it. I asked to see the letter. He showed it to me and it was true. He told me to be ready the next morning because a truck was going to the ghetto and I could go with the truck, he and I.

My happiness was unnatural. I was going to see my uncles and aunts. I was dancing on air. I ran to my friends and told them the news. Everyone was jealous that I was running away from hell. Some refused to talk to me. The whole night I couldn't sleep, watching through the window for the first sign of dawn. I imagined that I was already in the ghetto and my sick aunt was healthy again. I imagined that I got back on a good working brigade and that everything was fine. I could not help feeling, though, that something had happened to Aunt Ettel. I wouldn't let myself think about it. I hoped that I would return to find the situation better than when I left.

As the sun began to come up I got dressed quietly. I sat waiting. Every minute it got lighter. The other people began to get up and the barracks became filled with noise. One ran to wash, another to get some coffee; some were still in their bunk beds. We heard the order to line up on the field. The leader counted us quickly and told the German master to divide us into work groups.

I heard the column leader call out, "Hershke Gordon. Come out of the line." I ran up and he told me to return to the barracks and get ready to go back to the ghetto. "I am already ready to go, I said. I brought nothing here and I have nothing to take back."

But I had to return the two covers and the metal soup pail to the orderly in the camp.

After that, I ran back to the column leader in the barracks. He said we would leave as soon as the truck came. The time moved so slowly, but finally I saw the truck drive into the field. The German camp leader got into the cab with the driver. I rode with the column leader on top of the canvas cover in the bed of the truck. As we drove past the fence with its electric wires I started waving to the barracks.

"Who are you waving to?" the column leader asked.

"I am saying goodby to the barracks, which I hope I never see again. I am so happy to be going back to the ghetto where I will see my sick aunt and my other aunts and uncles. They won't even believe that I have come back from a working camp."

My companion listened and said, "You think it is such a great thing to be in the ghetto? The whole ghetto is standing on chicken legs. One nice morning it will be divided into different working camps or the whole ghetto will be taken to German concentration camps."

I knew very well that the fate of the ghetto was not good, but I was not interested in what happened to the ghetto. The main thing to me was that I would be with my family. "My mother and father I lost right at the beginning of the war. My only wish is to be with my uncles and aunts wherever they send us. I just hope they send us to one place, not one here and another there," I said.

He interrupted my words. "With me it is different. I don't have anybody in the ghetto. My wife and two children were shot and I was left in the ghetto by myself. I had a good friend in the Jewish Presidium, and thanks to him I got this job as column leader. I am pretty happy here. To me, it makes no difference if I am in the ghetto or in this camp. It doesn't matter what brigade I am in."

As we talked, the time flew. We had left the camp around ten in the morning and it was already one in the afternoon. My impatience began to grow again. I wanted to see the ghetto fence. We had to drive another two and a half hours, but we were halfway there.

Just as we began to get hungry the truck came to a standstill.

The German camp leader jumped out of the cab and went into a Lithuanian home. Soon a little farm girl came out carrying two big jugs of milk and a loaf of white bread. She gave me one jug and a big piece of bread and gave the column leader the other. We drank in a hurry and ate the bread.

As we started driving again, the column leader became more hopeful. "One day it is going to get better."

"You are never supposed to lose your hope," I told him.

Soon it was three o'clock and I could see the fenced-in ghetto. Every minute the ghetto became bigger as we got closer. We came to the Slobodka bridge from the side opposite Kovna. It was about 3:30 when we drove up to the ghetto fence. As we came to the gate by Krisciukaicio Street, I jumped off the truck to pass through the guarded gate.

Suddenly I had a terrified feeling. I wasn't scared about going through the gate, but I could no longer keep away the feeling that something had happened to my sick aunt. After the German commandant frisked me, I waited for the column leader to come through so I could say goodby. We wished each other good luck.

17. Back in the Ghetto

Here I was in the ghetto, but I was afraid to go home, feeling that a disaster awaited me. Whatever would be, I could not stay in the streets, I thought. I began walking faster, but my steps were uncertain. My heart was pounding. As I came close to my home and saw the little gray door, I came to a standstill. I could not go in.

I saw a woman coming toward me. I waited until the woman was close and I saw that she was our good neighbor, Mrs. Resnick. She said, "Hershke, is that you? How did you get here?"

I didn't answer but came back with a question. "Mrs. Resnick, do you know how my aunt is doing?"

"Your aunt is better," she said and walked away.

At this, I calmed down and was more sure of myself. I didn't hesitate at the door but opened it right up and walked into the house. The little kitchen where I used to sleep looked dark and empty. I ran into the other room where my aunt and uncle slept and found Uncle Abraham sitting on a chair with his head down. My aunt was not there.

I called out, "Uncle Abraham, where is Aunt Ettel?"

He jumped up and said, "Hershke, your second mother is dead."

I began to cry hysterically. "Why did God punish me so much that I couldn't be at my aunt's funeral?" I fell on my knees and put my head on the bed where she had been the last time I saw her. I couldn't forgive myself. I started shaking, and my uncle put some compresses on my forehead. I stayed this way for two hours.

When I came to my senses, my uncle told me what had happened after they took me out of the ghetto and sent me to the working camp.

The morning after I left he took my aunt to the hospital to get ready for an operation. The operation took four hours. Afterward my aunt started feeling better. She told the doctor that he could call her husband and her two sisters and their husbands. They came together, and she spoke a few sentences and said goodby to each one. As everyone left, she called to Aunt Golda and told her, "Golda, I won't live. If Hershula comes back from the work camp alive, take care of him. Be like a mother to him." With those words on her lips, her life ended.

"It has been ten days since she died," my uncle said, "and you and I are left without a wife and mother. Who is going to take care of us? After work now, since your aunt is gone, I go to Aunt Golda's to eat. She treats me well but she is only my sister-in-law, not a wife. I am not a young man anymore. No one knows how much we loved her. In good times and bad, we never fought or had arguments. But maybe this way is better; she has her peace now. Who knows what we will have to go through yet? Maybe we won't be able to have a peaceful death. If I had the strength, if I could commit suicide, I would have done it. This is the only thing that I cannot forgive God for—he should have taken me with her. My life without her is worth nothing. I am walking on God's earth like a useless animal. I eat at someone else's table."

Listening to his words, I began to shake again. Then I fell asleep for an hour. I woke up feeling a little better but with a terrible headache. My uncle was sitting next to me with his head hanging down and big tears like cherries falling from his eyes. When he saw that I was awake, he covered his eyes and said, "Tomorrow we are going to the ghetto cemetery and I will show you where your aunt is buried. Now I suppose you want something to eat."

My appetite was completely gone. My heart was heavy and tight. I was filled with new tragedy and I told Uncle Abraham that I could not eat.

He said, "If Aunt Golda and Aunt Celia knew that you were

back from the working camp, they would already be here. If you want, we can walk up to their homes."

"I will see them tomorrow," I told my uncle. I was so tired and griefstricken that I didn't even want to see my two aunts. "You should go to bed and relax. You will fall asleep and forget your troubles," I told him. I went off and let him get into bed. I brought my old chairs into the little kitchen and lay down, still dressed. Even though the chairs were too small for me and my legs were on the window, I still felt a difference from sleeping on the working camp floor. It did not take long for me to fall asleep.

When I awoke the next morning it was already ten o'clock. Uncle Abraham had made tea and was ready to eat. He gave me a glass of tea and a piece of bread, took the same for himself, and sat down next to me. The bread he gave me was yesterday's ration, since I did not have a ration card myself as yet. The tea was sweetened with saccharin that my uncle had gotten because he worked in the ghetto shops. As we finished the bread and tea, he spoke. "Hershke, now we are going to go the the cemetery and I will show you your aunt's grave."

We didn't talk at all as we walked; it was like the stillness before a storm. The cemetery was right in back of the ghetto shops on Varniu Street, surrounded by barbed wire two feet high. As I walked through the open gate I saw thousands of graves before me, so close to each other that it looked like one mass grave. The cemetery was too small and the dead ones too many. Even dead, they had no peace. Many graves were those of young people. Quite a few graves had grass growing over them and you could not see the grave, only the little wooden board with the family name. But we saw many widows pulling grass from their loved ones' graves as we walked.

Uncle Abraham stopped beside a little board that read "Ettel Gizelter." The ground was so fresh that not one blade of grass was growing.

I went down on my knees and cried, "It is me, Hershula. I came back from the working camp but I didn't find you. My lovely aunt, I will never in my life forget you. You will always be alive before me."

My uncle stood above me and his tears fell on the earth. He

bent down and picked me up from the grave and said, "That's enough, Hershke. Let's go."

Once more I kissed the ground and stood up. We started walking from the cemetery to Aunt Golda's. On the way I asked Uncle Abraham where he had gotten the money to put up such a nice board on Aunt Ettel's grave. He told me that he was paying for it with his rations, his marmalade, bread and soup.

"What are you eating then," I asked, "if you give everything away?"

"I cannot eat so much anyway."

"How much do you have to pay for that?" I asked him.

"Two big boxes of marmalade, five pounds of bread, and twenty-two rations of soup. I will be paid up in six months."

I thought to myself that if I could get in a good work brigade again like the potato brigade, I could pay up the whole thing at one time, but this was only a fantasy.

When we got to Aunt Golda's, she was standing by the kitchen. Her little boy, Baruch, sat on the table playing with his sister, Marska, who was standing by the table eating a raw potato.

Uncle Abraham said, "Hey Golda, look who is here." She turned around and saw me.

"Hershke," she cried as she hugged and kissed me with tears in her eyes. The little ones kissed me too. Aunt Golda and Marska let me go, but Baruch held onto my finger and pulled me to the chair. "Hersh," he said, "sit."

I sat down and he climbed in my lap as I asked Aunt Golda about Uncle Yenchik and his work. She told me that he was still working in the same place—in the kitchen of a German hotel—and every night he brought home a little extra soup and bread. In the meantime she put baked potatoes on the table and told me to eat. When Uncle Yenchik came home and saw me sitting at the table, he hugged me and we kissed each other. He hadn't believed he would ever see me again.

I told them the whole story of the working camp and how the Germans treated me. Everybody's eyes were filled with tears of joy, but also sorrow for my aunt's death. It was getting dark, so Uncle Abraham and I got up to go home. On the way we would stop and see Aunt Celia and Uncle Borach. As we left, Aunt Golda said, "God forbid, don't forget to come to supper tomorrow night."

We went a few hundred yards to Aunt Celia's. When we opened the door she and Uncle Borach stood stunned for a minute as if they didn't recognize me. Then Aunt Celia cried out and hugged me and again I told the whole story from beginning to end of how I got back. My aunt saw how tired I was and that, no matter how I tried, my eyes kept closing, so we left after a short time for home.

When my uncle woke me the next morning it was already light. He was in a hurry to go to work. For me it was a day filled with new troubles. I had to report to the employment office to get a work card and a ration card. I went into the Jewish Committee and reported to the head of employment, Mr. Pavel Margolis. He was sitting behind the desk with his hands on his big belly. As soon as I had the door open, he asked gruffly, "What do you want?"

I told him my name and where I had come from. He had already heard about me. "Wait here," he told me, "I will be right back." After fifteen minutes he returned and handed me a card and said, "This is your working card. You go to the airfield. With this same card you will get your rations." When I saw the card to the airfield, I said. "Mr. Margolis, I can't go back on the airfield. I just came back from a working camp because of my swollen leg. I won't be able to keep up with eighteen hours a day on the airfield. Maybe it is possible for you to get me a different card for a different brigade where I could get more food and also be able to help my old uncle?"

He looked at me for a moment, then he hollered at me. His face was red. His eyes were bloodshot like an animal ready to attack. "What do you think? You don't like your working card? You can go right back where you came from! You stinking Jew! How dare you stand up before me and tell me that you don't like the work I have given you. Don't you know who I am?"

"Yes," I said, "I know who you are, Mr. Margolis," This made him even angrier.

He started to spit fire from his mouth. "This is your working brigade. You report to the airport. You are going to work there until you die. Tomorrow morning I want to see you by the ghetto fence, and if not, you know what is going to happen to you." With that he ran out of the room. I too was happy when I saw the other side of his office door.

My hope had again vanished. I had thought that maybe this time I would get a better working brigade so I could help Uncle Abraham, but here I was right back where I started from. When I told my uncle the story after he came home from work, he tried to encourage me. But I knew that it would take a miracle to get me out of the airport brigade now.

The next morning at four I got up and dressed quickly and went to the ghetto gate where all the working brigades were being organized. I got into the airport brigade and heard Mr. Margolis screaming, "Everybody four in a row." He started counting. As he came to my line he looked at me and smiled.

Here started the same old story, the old ghetto life. Every morning at four I got ready to march to the airport where I had to work with a pickax all day hitting heavy stones. The German masters walked around with rubber hoses and beat everyone as much as they could without a why or a when. People fell dead like flies. The older Germans were trouble, but the young ones, the fifteen- and sixteen-year-olds, used to beat with everything they could find, and once they started they didn't stop until they saw that the man was dead. I couldn't wait for it to get dark, when we would be on our way back to the ghetto. At the cry "Everybody in line" we lined up in fours and went to the barracks where the tools were kept and put them all back in a line before we left. Then the master turned us over to the German guard who would take us back to the ghetto. Before we started home, we were counted again like animals. If everyone was there, except for the ones beaten to death by the Germans, we would begin the march home.

Every day there were dead ones, some beaten, some dead from heart attacks from exertion, some dead from hunger and pain. Those of us alive thanked God we could make it to the ghetto again another night. At eight in the evening I would eat my soup and my ration of bread and go to bed to rest for the next

Back in the Ghetto

day's work. While I tried to fall asleep, Uncle Abraham would talk to me, ask me questions, and tell me stories. I would fall asleep as he talked. Thus I suffered through each day, wondering if I would be coming back from the airport the next day or if I would be one of the dead ones.

A rumor began in the ghetto that the Germans needed more people for another work camp outside the ghetto. This working camp was to be in Riga, the capital of Latvia; it wasn't even in Lithuania. With this news a panic started. I decided to run away from the ghetto and go the the Lithuanian janitor who lived in our old house. I talked it over with Uncle Abraham and he encouraged me.

"What can you lose?" he said. "I have lost everything anyway. I don't care what the Germans do with me. But you, Hershula, you are young, and if it is possible for you to run away from the ghetto, you may be the only witness from the whole family. You will be able to take revenge for our innocent spilled blood."

I tried to help pick up his spirits. "As long as I am out of the ghetto, I will bring you food. Meet me by the ghetto fence each night." We decided on a place and time.

The next morning I hugged and kissed my uncle and told him to give my best wishes to the rest of the family. Then I left for the ghetto fence to go to work.

18. Escape from the Ghetto and Life with the Lithuanians

At the ghetto fence, all the working brigades were already standing in line waiting to go to work. I got into my brigade and waited nervously. We heard the cry that the airfield brigade should go through the gate. I moved quickly to the front lines as we marched through the gate. I asked the person in back of me to take off the yellow star. He did and gave the star to me. I tore the yellow star from my chest and waited for the right moment. As we came to the Slobodka bridge, my heart was pounding like an alarm clock; it felt like it would fly out of my chest. I shifted my eyes from left to right, watching for the moment when the German guard had his eyes on something else. It was a moment of life or death.

Lithuanians walked on the sidewalks of the bridge while we walked in the street. I jumped from the line onto the sidewalk. I was a Jew no longer; I was a Lithuanian, a free man. I was blond-haired and blue-eyed and looked more Lithuanian than Jewish, so I was able to mix with the Lithuanians until the airfield brigade disappeared down the road. At first I walked slowly then I began walking faster, thinking that I was free, a free human being. What a good feeling it was! For the first time since the Germans had come, I was walking on the sidewalk, not pushed along the street like an animal. I had forgotten how to walk like a human being, and like a child I had to learn again. I felt as if I had awakened from a long sleep.

Two German soldiers walked past me and I suddenly realized that I was not free yet. If I was caught here, my life would be worth nothing. I was about two kilometers from my old house, but even with my life hanging by a thread I wanted to keep walking through the little streets I had roamed as a boy. I remembered walking with my mother and father, with my uncles, aunts, and cousins, on Saturday afternoons. Not thinking now, I walked the same way as if by instinct. I saw fewer Lithuanians; the streets looked poor and lonely. I remembered that, before the war, every corner was smiling with an expression of invitation and from each home there came the aroma of food cooking, of gefilte fish and fresh baked bread. Now that had disappeared; it looked as if that time had never existed. All I could see were a few Lithuanians walking with their heads down and a few Lithuanian children with dirty faces.

I saw nearby the biggest synagogue in Kovno and suddenly had the urge to run up to the door and open it. It was locked. I looked through the windows and could see inside. Many different articles were lying on the floor; they must have been Jewish valuables. I moved from the window and started walking again. I stopped when I saw that I was not far from the home where I was born. The home of my childhood, I thought, for already at seventeen I felt like an old man. It was the place I had played with my cousins and friends after school. None were left. I was by myself and did not know what awaited me in my own home. My steps quickened and my heart pounded harder. I stood on the steps of my old home with trembling hands. I was afraid to knock for fear some Germans would open the door instead of the Lithuanian. I gathered my courage and knocked once, twice, three times. I heard steps after the third time and the door opened. It was the Lithuanian's daughter.

She asked me in Lithuanian what I wanted, so I told her that I had come to look over the house that I had lived in a long time ago. She had not recognized me. I must have looked half-dead from not enough food or sleep. She told me that her father was not in and that I couldn't look at the house now, that I should come back later.

"Do you know who I am?" I asked.

"No."

"Griske." She had called me by that name before the war.

When she heard that name her face changed color. For a minute, she didn't know what to say. She opened the door to the kitchen and told me to come in. Her mother was sitting there, an elderly lady.

"Do you know who this is?" Raisa asked her mother. She told her my name, but her mother still didn't believe her. She looked me over from top to bottom.

"How did you get here? How did you run away?"

I told her the whole story while the daughter started putting food on the table. The table was filled with all kinds of foods that I had not seen for ages. My mouth started watering. I paid no attention to what the Lithuanian woman said to me; my eyes were on the food. Without waiting for them to ask, I sat down and started putting food into my mouth. I wasn't chewing, just swallowing. They looked at me as if I was crazy. They didn't believe a human being could eat so fast. Soon only the dishes were left, completely clean. It was good to feel full. For once, I was satisfied. I could feel that I was heavy as I got up from the table.

I said to the daughter, "Now I would like to sleep."

She took me to my old bedroom where my old steel bed with wheels on the legs was waiting for me. I lay down and a wonderful feeling surrounded me. I was laying on a mattress instead of two chairs! I was not used to it any more and for a while my back hurt, but soon I fell asleep. When I woke it was about ten in the evening. I could hear a deeper Lithuanian voice in the kitchen. I got up, rubbed the sleep from my eyes, and went to the kitchen, where the Lithuanian janitor sat with his wife and daughter.

As I came into the room, he said, "Good evening my friend," and gave me his hand. He asked me about the rest of my family, and I told him who was in the ghetto and who had died. I described the situation in the ghetto, what we had to go through at the hands of the Germans and how I escaped. He told me that he had heard a little about what was going on, but he had not believed it. He told me that I would have to watch out for the neighbors; if they recognized me on the street they would tell the Germans and we would all be killed. He also feared a search. "That is why I will make a place for you in the attic," he said, "and will bring you food and water every day."

"I cannot stay in the attic day and night. I have to have a little fresh air."

"Maybe at night you can come down and go outside."

"Not maybe. I will have to. I told my uncle that, as long as I am a free man, I will help him with food. I cannot let him starve, and I hope, I believe, that you will help me. If you give me food I will deliver it to the ghetto. I cannot pay you now, but after the war I will pay for everything."

The Lithuanian didn't answer, but he told his daughter that tomorrow he would fix me a place in the attic.

In the morning I went into the attic and got on my bed. There were no windows, only some light coming through cracks in the wood. There was no one to talk to. I could hardly wait until the light rays disappeared. Slowly I opened the attic door and quietly went downstairs. When I got onto the street, I stopped and breathed the fresh air. I went back into the house, where the daughter and her mother had a sack packed for me. It was not big but it was well packed. I took it and asked for a bottle of whiskey.

"What do you need whiskey for?"

"I will need it to bribe the guard. Money I don't have, so this is the best medicine." She went to the buffet and took out a little bottle of whiskey for me. I put it in my pocket and left the house. It was already quite dark, about six or seven in the evening.

I moved toward the ghetto quickly, seeing here and there Lithuanians coming home from work. Otherwise there was a dead stillness. In the stillness I heard the tramping of heavy boots and understood that it was German soldiers. I met a number of soldiers, but they just walked past me. I thought, "God forbid if they should stop me and ask where I am going and ask me to show my papers." I could see the ghetto as I carried my sack to the point where I had arranged to meet my uncle. I saw a Lithuanian guard with a rifle on his shoulder marching up and down along the fence. I sat outside waiting and watching for my uncle. When I saw a man move three times by the fence, I could tell that it was Uncle Abraham. I ran up to the guard and told him in Lithuanian, "I have a very good friend, a Jew. I owe him a lot of favors. I want to give him some food through the fence." My Lithuanian was very good and he did not know that I was a Jew.

He began yelling that I wasn't supposed to do such things.

"You, a Lithuanian, are not supposed to even be here by the fence. I have a right to shoot you." I took out the little bottle of whiskey and put it in his hand. As soon as I did, he closed his mouth. He said just one thing, "Do it fast."

I gave the signal to my uncle and he came to the fence, lifting two wires so I could push the sack through. I asked him if anything had happened since I had left. He said, "No, but people are telling stories."

I didn't want to talk long so I told him I would see him the next night. When I got back to our house, the Lithuanians were sitting by the stove eating potato pancakes. They told me to sit down and tell them how everything had gone. I told them it had gone all right and that my uncle wanted me to thank them for what they were doing for us. I also had a good helping of pancakes before I went to the attic to sleep.

Stretched out on my bed, I couldn't understand what was going on with the Lithuanians. First they gave us over to the Lithuanian guerrillas to get rid of us, and now they were so nice to us. They were willing to hide me, to help me with food to take to the ghetto. A few days later the janitor opened up. He told me that right after the Jews were taken to the ghetto and locked up behind the fence, the Germans started going after the Lithuanians. They mobilized the young Lithuanians in the German army and sent them to the Russian front. They never came back. The older Lithuanian men were sent out on working brigades. The Lithuanians were no longer free either.

I understood then why he was so nice to me. When he lost some of his own freedom he began to understand what it was like for us. He wanted to make up for what he had done earlier. Maybe he realized that when the war was over and some of us were left alive, he would have to give an account of his actions. This way he would be able to say, "I helped a Jew. I hid him and helped him get food to the ghetto."

A few times when no one was home, I came down from the attic into the house and turned on the radio. An English station broadcasting in Lithuanian gave the latest news. When I heard that the Germans were having trouble and that the Russians were advancing and the Americans were bombarding many

German cities, I rejoiced. I would tell my uncle the latest developments when I took my sack of food to the ghetto. This news was better than the food. The murderers were paying for the blood they had spilled.

After four or five weeks I started feeling that I was in a worse position than if I were in the ghetto. In the day I could not see the light. I had to keep still and listen to every movement, every step. My eyes became accustomed to the dark until I could see better at night than in the day. I wondered if I would go blind. I was never hungry now, and I didn't have to work at the airport, but those were the only benefits. In the ghetto I was with Jews and friends and relatives. I had someone to talk to. Here I just sat waiting for a miracle or for the war to be over. I was so depressed. I came to the conclusion that food and work weren't that important anymore. I didn't want to be any better than the other Jews who lived in the ghetto, who were awaiting their fate. "What will happen to them will happen to me," I thought. I decided that in the next few days I would return to the ghetto.

I planned to tell Uncle Abraham that night when I took him the food that I would come back to the ghetto the next night, but I had a funny feeling that I should not go to see him that night. It was as if something told me, "Hershke, don't go tonight, not tonight." I didn't let the thought stay in my head. I was halfway to the ghetto when I heard two German soldiers walking behind me. I walked slower so that they would pass, but when they came up to me they stopped.

One asked in German, "Lithuanian, please tell me where is such-and-such street."

I wanted to answer, but my voice stuck in my throat. Luckily I didn't lose my composure. I told them that I didn't know exactly. The other German asked me what I was carrying in my sack and I answered that it was the food I got from work. When they asked where I was going so late, I told them that I lived not too far from here and was on my way home. Inside, my whole body was shaking. Thank God I got rid of them. As they walked away, I began breathing normally again and continued on my way.

When I reached the ghetto, I could see that something wasn't right. The whole fence was lit up with huge floodlights, and German and Lithuanian guards were running back and forth like mad dogs. I hid in the entry of a house right across from the ghetto and waited feverishly to see if I could spot my uncle walking on the other side of the fence. It is a good thing that I didn't see him, because I couldn't have given him the food anyway. The ghetto was lit as if it was the middle of the day; if we had been seen, we would have been shot. I waited ten or fifteen minutes before I started walking back to my house. I knew that some new kind of massacre was going on in the ghetto, for I had heard screaming. They must have been taking people from the houses. I was afraid my uncles and aunts would be victims. I would have to delay my return to the ghetto.

When I came back to the house with my sack of food, the Lithuanian janitor asked me what had happened. I told him that my uncle hadn't come to the fence and that there would be new killings in the ghetto. I ate nothing but went right to the attic. But I couldn't wait until the next morning. I ran down to the Lithuanian and told him that I had to go out in the street and find out what was happening in the ghetto.

"You cannot go," he told me. "What if the Germans catch you or my neighbors see you? The Germans would kill us all. You quiet down and sit in the house and I will go find out what is happening." He was gone a long time. When I heard him open the door I ran to him, I was so anxious.

With his head hanging, he told me, "Griske, the Germans took Jews from the ghetto. How many, we don't know. They are taking them to Riga. That is what the Lithuanians told me, and this is all I can tell you."

The next night I took my sack of food and ran to the ghetto. It looked as if it was back to normal again. There weren't so many floodlights and there were single guards again. There was a dead stillness in the ghetto. I thought that Uncle Abraham wouldn't come that night. He might have been taken; I didn't know. I waited for a while and saw that on the ghetto side of the fence there was a dark shadow marching around. I ran to the fence and called, "Uncle."

He came to the wires and pulled up the bottom two so I could push the sack through. I was so happy to see him that I didn't know what to ask.

He told me that the Germans had taken a thousand Jews to deport to the labor camps in Riga. But thank God my other uncles and aunts were still together in the ghetto. I wanted to come back that night, but the deportation made me wait one more night.

When I told my uncle that I was coming back, he said to me, "Why do you want to come back and put a healthy body in a sick bed? You are a free man."

"I don't have time to tell you, but I will see you tomorrow night. I will come back with the airport brigade." I left and went back to the house. The Lithuanians were waiting to find out what had happened. When they saw that I did not have the sack of food, they knew that my uncle was still in the ghetto. As we sat eating at the table, I told them that I would be leaving. The janitor became upset. "Why do you want to go back to the ghetto? Aren't we treating you right? Don't we give you enough food?"

"You have given me plenty to eat and have treated me very well, but you have to understand that food and drink are not everything. I want a little breathing space. I want to walk around in the daylight. Here I have to stay in the attic all day and be afraid of every movement I hear. This also is not life, and that is why I have decided to go back to the ghetto." The Lithuanian, his wife, and daughter looked at me in silence and I understood that they knew what I meant. I went up to the attic to bed.

The next evening I went down to eat my last supper as a free man. Dinner was waiting on the table, a holiday dinner with whiskey. On the floor was a sack of food waiting for me. When we finished eating I said goodby to each of them and thanked them dearly for helping me.

I left and walked quickly to the Slobodka bridge to make sure I caught the working brigade as it returned from the airport. Soon I saw them coming. I darted into line and put my yellow star on in front, asking the man behind me to put on the one in back, and I was a Jew again.

As we came to the fence, the guards started inspecting the first few lines, looking to see what they had in their sacks, but they checked only the first few before they told us to run through the gate.

19. A New Work Brigade

As I came through the gate I could see Uncle Abraham waiting for me. He was so happy to see me, so impatient, that he couldn't wait until we got home to start asking me questions.

"Hershke, why did you come back to the ghetto so soon? What happened? Did the Lithuanian throw you out?" I explained my reasons to him and he told me that I had picked a good day to come back. Since they had deported so many people the day before, the ghetto leadership didn't know who was taken and who was left, so they wouldn't ask me any questions. I would be able to get a different working card because everyone had to get a new card.

The next morning I went to the ghetto fence. I saw two Jewish police running around looking for people to go to work. They ran up and grabbed me by the arm. I didn't know where they were pulling me, but they took me to a small brigade with four men and one woman and told me to stay there. I didn't even have time to ask where we were going before I heard the order to move. As we went through the fence, one man, who saw that I was startled, told me not to worry. He told me that this was a good brigade; I would get plenty to eat and would not have to work too hard.

It was called the police order brigade and the leader was named Rabinovich. When we came to the place where we would work, we went into a basement where there was a stove. The woman's job was to cook for us. Our leader went upstairs with the German officers who were living there in order to find out what kind of work they had for us that day. He came down and told us that we would have to move some furniture. Another man and I started carrying chairs and the other two moved tables from one room to another. At noon we went to the basement to eat the soup and bread the woman had ready for us. We could eat as much as we wanted and take the rest home with us. The other workers knew about it so they had big cans to carry soup in. I had nothing, so I ate everything I could. After we ate we went back to work until five o'clock. At five we were taken back to the ghetto, and each went home in a different direction.

When I got home and told my uncle about the brigade I had gotten that day, he asked me several times if I was kidding. He couldn't believe I had had so much luck on my first day back in the ghetto. I made sure I had a big container for soup the next morning.

Our work the second day was to move the tables and chairs back to the place they had been the day before. We thought they just wanted to make us miserable. Someone asked them why we were working like this and got the answer that they needed us for their reports. Germans who could show they had Jews working for them wouldn't be sent to the Russian front. Each week they sent in reports that the Jews were producing and they were needed to supervise. In reality nothing was accomplished; they just wanted to save their own skins. At the same time, as long as the Germans were keeping people from the ghetto working, the ghetto was being kept alive and not liquidated.

So it went. One day the work was a little harder; the next, a little easier. We could have lasted until the war was over if they had let us sit there.

One evening, when I came home from work, Uncle Abraham said, "Did you hear the latest news? People are saying they are going to bring German Jews into our ghetto."

"This is pretty good news," I said. "Better that they put people in instead of taking people out."

Nobody would believe it. Why would they bring German Jews to our ghetto? Why would they take Jews out of our ghetto and then bring in others from some other place? With the Germans, anything was possible; they wanted to keep us in suspense so we wouldn't know if we were coming or going.

A New Work Brigade

The day did arrive when they brought the German Jews, but not into our ghetto. They brought them into Lithuania to kill them. They came by train in regular passenger cars, thinking they were being moved to the Slobodka ghetto. When they arrived at the station in Kovno, the Germans put them in trucks and took them to the Ninth Fort to machine gun them down. To get to the Ninth Fort, they had to pass our ghetto. We stood by the fence and saw how they took our brothers and sisters to slaughter. They rebelled, we found out later.

Jews from our ghetto helped them unload their baggage at the station in Kovno. They could see that the Germans were wearing their best furs and jewelry, and their suitcases were tagged to be taken to the Slobodka ghetto. The German Jews asked the Lithuanian Jews how much farther it was to the ghetto. Two days later, the Germans brought all their clothing, the boots and coats and furs, to us in the ghetto to be sorted, and we understood that the German Jews were alive no longer.

Everyone said that the dead were better off than the living. We were so demoralized. Everyone walked around in the ghetto like a dead shell of a person. Our willpower had disappeared so completely that we didn't even have a thought of rebelling. That is what the Germans wanted.

In the evening, at about 8:30, as we came out from the house, we could see a fire rising from the direction of the Ninth Fort. We knew that the Germans were burning Jewish bodies.

20. Red Plantation

On April 15, 1943, an order came from the Gestapo to the Jewish Presidium that they should get ready one hundred healthy working men to be taken to a working brigade. If they didn't come up with the men, the Germans would take the Jewish police. You can imagine how scared the Jewish police were, so they started making lists right away, reporting people like me with no parents or connections, not caring whether they were healthy or not. They just wanted to save themselves.

When the lists were ready, they went looking for the people on the lists. They began at two in the morning, so we were sleeping when we heard a knock on the door. Uncle Abraham got up, scared, and asked who was there. We thought it might be the Germans. They answered that it was the Jewish police and that we should open the door. They came in, took out a list, and asked for Hersh Gordon and told me to dress and go with them.

Uncle Abraham said, "Why do you always pick on my nephew? He just came back not long ago from one working camp and now he has to go again? Why don't you take someone else? He is a young kid. How long do you think he can hold up like this, going from one camp to another?"

"What do you want us to do," the police answered, "go in his place?"

I knew very well what my uncle would like to have replied, but he didn't say it. He was thinking, "It wouldn't be so bad if they would try one of the working camps instead of living like parasites on someone else's blood." But if he had said anything, they would have taken him, too.

I dressed quickly and said goodby. The police took me to the

Red Plantation

ghetto fence where there was another ghetto jail. In this particular jail they usually kept people arrested for not going to work or for coming late to work. I went into a big room where there were a lot of people. They were asking each other, "Did you hear where they are taking us?" No one knew. We asked the police guarding us, but they didn't know either. Every minute more and more were brought in. Each was trying to guess where we would be taken. One said the Ninth Fort; another said he heard from a good source that we were being taken to Germany to work because with all the Germans fighting on the fronts they needed people to take over their jobs.

I met a friend of mine here named Pascha Schmidt. He asked me, "Hershke, do you think they are going to take us to work in Germany?"

I told him, "In ten hours, we will all be older and we will know where they are taking us."

It began to get light outside. At 6:00 AM the Germans drove up in trucks with Ukrainian volunteers on them, a Ukrainian SS. The Jewish police told us to get in lines of four abreast, counted us, and told us to get in the truck. The Ukrainians gave the order and we started moving.

We were packed like cattle in the trucks, with no room to move. We couldn't wait for the moment when the trucks would stop. They finally did stop in a big field. We jumped off the trucks and stood in line again to be counted. As we stood in line, anyone who tried to stretch or move a little after the ride was beaten by the Ukrainians with their rifles, or kicked in the shins by their boots. They hit and kicked us even if we didn't do anything, and this was only the beginning of our lives at Red Plantation, near Vyzuonos.

After they finished counting they took us up to a pig stall and told us we would sleep there. It looked like the pigs had been moved out only a few hours before; manure lay in big piles. They put us to work cleaning out the stall so we would be able to sleep there that night. There were no lights, only a few gas lamps. We couldn't wait for dark when we could hide ourselves in the stall to escape the brutal Ukrainians. They were ten times as bad as the Germans.

There was a dead stillness among us. Everyone thought that

this would be the last working brigade we would be in. No one would come out alive from this one. As we went to sleep, the Ukrainians came in hollering and told us to get up, hitting us with their rifles. It was 4:00 AM. We couldn't even finish putting on our clothes as we ran onto the big field, one in one shoe and another with one arm in his shirt.

They counted us again and divided us into groups to go to work. We had to drag cement and carry bricks and dig holes. We were building barracks for the Ukrainian SS. Each had to carry fifty pounds of cement or bricks on his shoulder. As we worked, they would hit or kick us whenever they could.

After the first day of work they gave us a ration of bread for a week, two pounds. That wasn't enough for such hard work. Every day we worked until 10:00 PM. At noon we would get a can of soup; they called it soup but we called it warm water. With this kind of food we had to work and hold up through all the troubles. It went on this way for a couple of months. Every day our group got smaller as people died. I too began to grow weaker.

One morning when we went to work, I could hardly wait for noon when we would get our soup. When I got into the soup line, I was the last one and right in front of me was my friend Pascha. As we were about to get the soup, we heard a rifle shot and my friend cried, "My arm! My arm!" and started running. He fell onto the ground and there was panic. Everyone ran toward the pig stall. As I ran I felt that I could not move my left arm. I felt it and it was wet. I tore off my sleeve and saw that my arm was soaked in blood. It felt like it was being pricked with needles.

One Ukrainian had tried to shoot me, but the bullet went through my arm and hit my friend's arm. It hit his bone and exploded (it was a hollow headed bullet), so that it tore off his arm. He was lying on the ground with blood around him. People ran up and tried to tie his arm with a cloth to stop the bleeding. When I saw him, I thought my arm was gone, too, but I didn't lose control.

I washed my arm, wrapped it tightly with my shirt, and waited to see what would happen. Right away the leader of the Ukrainians came up and said to us, my friend and me, that he was sending us back to the ghetto. In this bad luck was a little good luck for me. For Pascha, it was a big loss; he lost his arm. They took us both back to the ghetto, about two and a half hours away. Pascha went to the hospital, where they amputated his arm. Later, when the Germans had the children's massacre, Pascha was killed too. The doctor cleaned my wound, put a bandage on it and put my arm in a sling. I was told not to move my arm around, and I went back to my uncle.

21. The *Obersturmbannführer*

By the time I got home from the hospital, it was already dark. I knocked on the door before entering. When Uncle Abraham saw me, he cried out emotionally "Hershula is here!" As he told me to sit down and take off my jacket, he realized that my left sleeve was empty. I told him that a Russian guard had shot me and for that reason they had sent me home. He looked at me with wondering eyes and said, "It is a miracle! A miracle has happened. You have come back alive, back from the dead, alive! You should do a lot of praying." He also said that I looked so worn out that, if he hadn't known me so well, he would have had difficulty recognizing me. He gave me something to eat.

After I ate I went to bed while he went to tell the other aunts and uncles the good news. The next morning, since I had a furlough from the doctor for a whole week, I walked around the ghetto visiting with friends and relatives. My aunts were happy to see me and each gave me something to eat.

One evening later in the week when I got home, Uncle Abraham was already there fixing supper. He ran about nervously, not saying anything, so I knew something was wrong. "Hershula," he finally said, "not long ago there was a Jewish policeman here asking where you were. I told him you were not here and that if he had anything to tell you, to tell me and I would give you the message. So he said that the ghetto commander, Mr. Goecke, got a letter from the leader of the Russian SS where you worked that the Ukrainian guard shot you and your friend because you were trying to escape. He wanted you and Pascha to appear before him for an investigation, but since

The *Obersturmbannführer*

Pascha is in the hospital and can't come you should appear before the commandant by yourself."

When I heard that story, everything became dark. The guard had made up an excuse for shooting me to save himself. I began to shiver all over like chattering teeth. This commandant was the biggest murderer we knew. He had already on his hands the blood of thousands of Jews. In 1939, he was the leader of the German concentration camp at Dachau. He had gotten his big title of *Obersturmbannführer* by killing so many blameless souls. I had to appear before that murderer and defend myself.

I could not sleep that night. I tossed from side to side and wished that the investigation were over and it was life or death, not this waiting. What could I tell him? How could I persuade him that I hadn't tried to run away? I was just a little Jew. Such thoughts ran through my mind all night. It seemed to last a year; every five minutes I would look through the windows to see if it was getting light.

At nine in the morning, the Jewish policeman came to take me to the commandant. His office was right by the ghetto fence on Varniu Street. The closer we got to that office, the harder my heart pounded. As I climbed the steps my legs were shaking. I even saw stars before my eyes. The policeman, seeing me looking like I was drunk, caught my arm and helped me up the steps. When we came to the door, he told me to wait in the hall while he went in to say that he had brought the "criminal."

I went into the room, and there was the murderer sitting behind a big desk. Right out he asked me, "Is it true that you and your friend wanted to run away from the camp? Look me in the eye!" As I looked in his eyes, I could feel that it was like an x-ray machine. It was as if he could tell everything that was in me. He had the eyes of a cutthroat. Eyes like that I had never seen before.

The answer stuck in my throat. I stammered out in German, "Nein."

His second question was, "How long will you have to go around with your arm bandaged?"

I said I didn't know.

"Your new work will be right here in the ghetto, in my office. You may leave."

When I was on the other side of the door, I started breathing a little easier. I was in a cold sweat, wringing wet. I began running like crazy toward home. When I got home I fell on my uncle's bed and went to sleep.

When Uncle Abraham came home from work and found me he was so happy he didn't know what to ask me. He had thought that he would see me no more. I told him everything the commandant had said and I was still trembling. This convulsion kept up for several days.

When I was no longer scared, I began walking around the ghetto streets again. My arm was getting better after two weeks of doing nothing, and the doctor told me that I should start exercising with light work. I went to the Presidium to Mr. Rabinovitz, who was handing out the working cards, and he gave me a card to go to work in the German commandant's office. The work was easy, chopping wood and moving furniture. I had to report to work at eight in the morning and work until four in the afternoon. It was a lot easier than going to the airfield. I also got a little more food to eat.

At this time, the Germans were getting beaten on the Russian front and began pulling back from Russian territory. When we heard this news in the ghetto we rejoiced. But at the same time, we began to wonder what would happen to us. We knew the Germans pretty well, and we knew that when they pulled back from Lithuania, one of two things would happen. Either they would take us to Germany or they would set fire to the ghetto and burn us with it. This is what really happened. Those who volunteered to go with them to Germany were sent to the concentration camps. Many tried to hide in the ghetto, so they set it on fire. Maybe one hundred or one hundred and fifty survived, hiding in the ghetto until the Russians came. Ninety percent of the Jews in the ghetto thought the Germans would be so occupied with getting themselves out of Lithuania they would forget about the ghetto, but this did not happen. They were too well organized.

Many Jews started getting ready for that moment when the

Germans would leave. Some, as soon as it got dark, started digging holes under the basements or under their homes. We called them moles. They made places where they could hide themselves until the Germans gave up and left. Every house that had a cellar was trying to camouflage the hole so the Germans wouldn't be able to find it. Many built tunnels so they could come out in the house or at the street. People began storing some of their rations there for later use. Some even put in ventilation and electrical lighting, but not all could afford such luxury. Uncle Yenchik had camouflaged his cellar and was hoping it would save his family.

In the meantime life went on, with everybody going to work each day and the Germans looking for more men to go to the airfield; they were enlarging it. I went on working in the German commandant's office. As long as we were all working, we were not as scared. But suddenly a dark cloud came over the ghetto again. On Sunday, March 26th, 1944, in the evening, the German commandant, Mr. Goecke, told the Jewish police that at 8:00 AM the next day they should be ready in full dress uniform in front of his office. He was going to issue new orders about protecting the ghetto from air attacks.

22. The Liquidation of the Helpless

On the morning of Monday, March 27, 1944, all the working brigades went to work at the airfield, in the workshops, and in the city and the ghetto. The only ones left home were the people working night shifts, the old people, the sick, the young, and some mothers. When all the brigades were out at work, about 8:30 in the morning, more guards appeared around the ghetto fence. This was not a good sign for the ghetto, but until this moment no one had thought anything bad would happen because everyone had gone to work. But this was a new German tactic; while everyone was at work, the murderers would come into the ghetto homes and take the children. This way they wouldn't have to look so hard for them.

At the same time the Jewish police were meeting in the commandant's yard. At 8:00 they were all in line ready to listen to the new orders. Commandant Goecke came out with a big group of SS German guards. They surrounded the police and ordered all of them to sit on the ground. Buses started driving into the ghetto. The windows were painted so you couldn't see in or out. A German taxi with a bullhorn started driving through the ghetto streets telling everyone, "Attention! Attention! Everybody has to stay home. Whoever leaves the house for even a few steps will be shot." The Jewish policemen were ordered to crawl on all fours to get into the buses. One policeman by the name of Levner got so scared that his legs cramped and he couldn't crawl onto the bus. He was shot right there. When they realized they were going to be taken to the Ninth Fort, they thought they would be killed. Two other policemen jumped out of the bus and were also shot.

When they arrived at the Ninth Fort, the Germans took everything away from them, their clothes and everything else, and beat them to a pulp. After this they were taken to the bunkers and there appeared before them the famous mass killer, Mr. Kittel. He tried various methods to find out from the police who had made hidden cellars and where they were. He also tried to find out about the young people, eighteen to twenty, who were trying to escape from the ghetto and contact the partisans in the woods.

The police revealed nothing. The first one they took for interrogation was the chief of the Jewish police, Moshe Levin. After him they took his assistant, Greenburg, and another man named Yehuda Zupovitz. Kittel started the interrogation by breaking their fingers, but he could get nothing from them. Later it was said that Police Chief Levin had made a pact with his officers not to reveal anything. But most people knew better than to tell the police anything they might later use to save their own hides. Kittel shot all three of them, and their bodies were burned later with the rest.

During this time masses of German Gestapo and Ukrainians were running from house to house in the ghetto throwing people out on the street. Everyone knew a liquidation had begun, but what kind no one knew. I saw from the window at work that the Germans and Russians were pulling children from the houses, even some my age. The old and the sick they forced into the buses with painted windows. There they were gassed with carbon monoxide. The screaming and crying tore at my heart. The Germans began playing music through the loudspeakers to cover up the screams coming from the helpless victims all over the ghetto.

When I realized what was happening, I thought of my aunts, and that they would lose their minds if something happened to their children. My Aunt Golda wouldn't know what to do with her husband at work. So I left my job and ran to her house to help hide the children. On every street there were guards with guns ready to shoot, but I hid from them, jumping over fences and taking alleys through the ghetto. I ran like a deer.

When I reached my aunt's house, I opened the door and said, "Quick, hide the kids!" I opened the door to the cellar and threw my cousins down into it with my aunt. I closed the trap door and covered it with a rug and put a table over that. It looked like nothing had happened and that everyone was at work. I couldn't get to my other aunt's house so I started working my way back to the commandant's office, hoping to get back before anyone noticed I was gone.

On the way I saw a German guard pulling a young man holding a little baby in his hands. As he got to the bus, he told the man to throw the baby into the bus. The man was so scared that he ran up to the leader of the German Gestapo and begged him not to take his child away. The leader said to him in a heavy voice, "If you don't throw the kid in with the rest, you will go with him." The father pretended that he didn't understand, so he asked him again to let him go back with his child. I could see that the leader's face was getting red. He pulled out his gun and shot at the father, but the gun jammed. The Gestapo leader told the man to go home.

I also saw a few mothers with little children that the Germans were pulling to the trucks. When they got there, the Germans ripped the children from their mothers' arms and threw them onto the buses. If the mothers wouldn't let go, the Germans set police dogs on them who bit the mothers until they passed out and dropped their children. A few mothers wouldn't let go even when the dogs bit them, so the Germans shot them right there or pushed them in with the children. Everyone on the buses was gassed.

As people figured out what was going on, the young and old started hiding themselves. Those who had no cellars hid in closets or under beds. Some hid small children between the pillows on the beds. But when the Germans came in they tore the house apart. If they thought there might be a false wall, they started knocking the wall out. They came equipped with axes, crowbars, and even small explosives.

About five in the evening people started coming back from their working brigades, and the Germans and Russians disap-

The Liquidation of the Helpless

peared from the ghetto. You can imagine what happened when the fathers and mothers came back from work. There was hardly a home in the ghetto where someone wasn't missing. People tore their hair out, people had heart attacks. Those who were left didn't know how to comfort the others. Mothers screamed, "Where is our God? How could he let such a killing happen? For such innocent souls, stones would cry." Everyone was completely hopeless, demoralized. Everyone was crying that he wished he had been there and been taken too. We wondered what would happen the next day. Would the murderers come back? What a night we went through in the ghetto.

The next morning many people didn't want to go to work in case the Germans came back because they had run out of time and hadn't gotten to all the houses. No one knew if the liquidation was finished or not. Everyone tried to hide their children and the old and sick who were left. When the airfield brigade left, a lot of kids and old people went with it to work. They were happy to escape for this time from the murderers' hands. The second liquidation started around 8:00 AM. The police were still being held in the fort. This time they brought bloodhounds and started looking again in the houses. They didn't just pull out the old and sick and young; they took everyone they found hiding. They took them from the ghetto to the Kovno railroad station, where they loaded them on trains and sent them to Auschwitz.

Taxis started driving through the ghetto with Gestapo in them, sitting with a few Jewish police who were showing them hiding places they knew of. Later it was shown that Kittel had used provocative brainwashing techniques until some of the police could no longer stand it. But very few actually broke down. The main informer here was named Benno Liptser. He was already cooperating with Mr. Kittel, and they only pretended to beat him. With his help, Kittel tried to break the morale of all the arrested Jewish police.

Even with all this, quite a few young people were able to hide until the Russians came. My aunts, Golda and Celia, were successful in hiding their children, but only for a short time, until the ghetto was liquidated. Then they were sent, with others who were left, to the concentration camps.

Those who survived were not to be envied. They had to stay

hidden all the time, not only from the Germans but also from their neighbors. Some Jewish mothers who had lost their children were so crazy with grief that if they saw other people's kids, they would run up to the guards and tell them children were hiding in that house. This is the way life went after the liquidation of the young and old and sick.

23. The Partisans in the Woods

A few days after the liquidation, everything that had happened to the police in the Ninth Fort came out. One hundred and thirty policemen had survived. Mr. Kittel kept forty in the fort and let ninety go back to the ghetto. The forty he kept were the higher ranking police, the captains and sergeants. They were eventually shot at the Ninth Fort. He tried to get information out of them and got money and valuables from their families as ransom, but didn't let any of them go. After he shot them, their clothes were brought back to the ghetto to be sorted.

Even though the police had been made to suffer like the rest of us, people did not forget their many betrayals, their cruelty to other Jews, and their favored status. Some of the people who survived the war, if they found a Jew who had been a policeman, went to the Russian court and told them about their work. The Russian court gave the police fifteen to twenty-five years in jail or in Siberia. In the first few weeks after the end of the war, some Jews terrorized the police, beating and killing any policeman they could find.

The Germans disbanded the Jewish police after the liquidation and substituted order keepers. The police had been under the control of the Presidium, but the order keepers were chosen by and under the orders of the German ghetto commandant and the Gestapo. The former police were given different jobs. The ghetto fences were guarded more heavily so that the Jews wouldn't be able to escape.

Even with all this close watching, Jews still tried to get in touch with sympathetic Lithuanians and the partisans in the woods so that when the moment came they could try to run from the ghetto and hide out with the Lithuanians. Parents who still had their children tried to get in touch with any Lithuanian friends as fast as they could, not just those in the cities but also those in the country. Many parents paid large sums of money, but again some Lithuanians took the children and then turned them in. Then both the children and the parents were killed.

A lot of young people started escaping from the ghetto into the woods. The leader of the underground in the ghetto was Chaim Yellin. He was a young man from Kovno who, before the war, had belonged to the Communist party. He was one of the Jewish intellectuals and belonged to a group of writers. He was tall and slim and about thirty years old. He had distinguished himself by taking Jews out of the ghetto to the Lithuanian partisans who were resisting the Germans. He was a hero.

Until he came, everyone in the ghetto had to try to get in touch with the partisans by themselves. They ran into a lot of trouble and fell into the hands of the Germans. He was the only one who tried to build up a communication system between the two groups. He had a communication network over a four-hundred-mile radius. The partisans were in the Rudninkai forest about sixty miles away. He got in touch with them, and the question of their location was finally answered. Before, many people ran away but didn't know where to go. The partisans were ready and willing to accept young people from the ghetto.

It was a large undertaking. Every night Yellin would organize people. He worked carefully so that the order keepers wouldn't find out. Everything was done in tight secrecy. I wanted to leave the ghetto and had gotten in touch with the underground; that is how I learned about Chaim Yellin.

He was never afraid. He used to walk around in Kovno like a Lithuanian whenever he wanted to. He disguised himself as a railroad executive. He always carried two guns in his pockets. During the last days of the ghetto, he was outside more than he was in. The whole organization of young people who wanted to escape was in his hands. Kittel somehow found out about Yellin, that he was the leader of the underground in the ghetto, and decided to catch him no matter what the cost. One morning, at the beginning of April, Yellin was walking on an errand in a Lithuanian street with a Lithuanian who was an undercover agent for the Germans. When the agent tried to stop him, Yellin, who had been in the business long enough to know what was going on, took out his revolver and shot the agent.

With all the commotion of the shooting, German and Lithuanian soldiers ran after him, hoping to catch him alive. He disappeared, jumping over fences and running down alleys until he reached the house of a Lithuanian friend who would hide him. As he ran into the house, a German officer saw him and tried to stop him, along with a Lithuanian policeman. Yellin shot at both of them and ran away again, hiding in a cellar not far from his friend's house. The Germans, knowing he couldn't be far away, brought in reinforcements and bloodhounds.

As they came to the cellar, Yellin knew he would fall into their hands. Since he was out of ammunition he tried to commit suicide with a razor blade, cutting his wrists. The Gestapo found him, very nearly dead, and arrested him. Kittel tried to keep him alive so he could get information out of him. There was a rumor in the ghetto that Yellin planned to take Kittel to the partisans' location in the woods, hoping to escape and take Kittel captive. But we came to understand that Kittel, no matter how much he wanted to find the partisans, didn't want to get too near them. Yellin would not give them the information, so they killed him.

After this the Gestapo tightened their hold on the ghetto. They tried to get hold of the new leaders of the partisans in the ghetto. Somehow the Gestapo got names of couriers and began arresting people. The remaining couriers had to leave quickly before their luck ran out.

On Saturday, April 14, 1944, at 9:00 PM a group of twelve men and women escaped from the ghetto. They got into a truck they had hired from a Lithuanian. As they came onto the Slobodka bridge and were almost to Jonavos Street, the Lithuanian chauffeur slowed down, complaining that the motor wasn't working right. Afraid that something was wrong, they got their ammunition and guns ready for any surprises. Suddenly the chauffeur stopped the truck and said he had to get out and look at the motor. When he did, machine guns started firing from all sides. The chauffeur had informed on the partisans and cooperated with the Germans. The Jewish men and women killed the chauffeur and started answering the German fire. Eight young people were killed, but four escaped with guns and ammunition in hand. They were lost to the Germans and reached the partisans in the woods. Two were lucky enough to survive the war.

After this incident, the underground group in the ghetto was completely paralyzed. They couldn't reestablish contact with the partisans. I had decided to run away from the ghetto and try to reach the partisans, but I didn't have time.

24. Kazlu Ruda and Escape

The situation in the ghetto worsened every day as the German losses on the Russian front grew and the Germans took out their disappointment on us. Rumors began to spread in the ghetto that the Germans would take the whole ghetto and put us in isolation, making us wear striped clothing like prisoners. When the Germans told the Jewish Presidium to get three to four hundred healthy men and women ready to go to work, it was the end of April, a Thursday night. Two order keepers came to my house and told me to go with them. My uncle got very upset. He asked them, "Where now?"

"Kazlu Ruda," they told him, "to dig peat."

Uncle Abraham held me in his arms and started crying. "This time," he said to me, "Hershula, this time I am pretty sure that we will not see each other again." He had lost his will and was completely drained. He suddenly seemed very old and frail. I started to encourage him.

"Uncle, we are going to see each other. I came back from a lot of other working brigades and I will come back from this one, too." At the same time, I too felt that we wouldn't see each other again. As I left the house, I turned around several times to look back, to look at the gray door of the house where we had lived. I never saw Uncle Abraham again. I don't even know where he was killed or what happened to him.

They put us on the trucks and took us out of the ghetto to the working camp, about 20 miles south, where there were already wooden barracks ready for us with two lines of bunk beds. The camp was surrounded by a high metal fence and guarded outside by mostly German guards, with a few Russians among them. Their offices and barracks were outside the camp, which was in the middle of a forest. The work was very hard; we worked fifteen or sixteen hours a day. There was little food, but one thing that helped was that the guards weren't as brutal as some of the others had been. At night, when we sat in the barracks eating our rations, the Russian guards would come in with their guitars, accordians, and mouth harmonicas and would sit down and start singing Russian songs for us. There was something about it; even though we were hungry and tired, no matter how bad we felt, we would find ourselves singing with them.

One nice summer morning when some of the people from our camp went to the ghetto to bring back food and supplies, they also brought back big news. A lot of people had been sent from the ghetto to small working camps around Kovno, in Aleksotas, Panemune, and other places. The people left in the ghetto were wearing striped clothing. We called them Sing Sing uniforms. We at the working camp were still wearing civilian clothes. Our German leader didn't seem too concerned about it. At the same time, the Russian guards were telling us political news, that the English and Americans had opened up a new front and that the Russians were attacking the Germans harder and harder. They said that the end of the war was not far away. The question was, what would happen to us?

Would they let us sit in the camp until the war was over, or kill us, or take us to a camp in Germany? Everyone felt that the end was near, but we all wanted to know what would happen to us. In Yiddish there is a saying: "The happiness is on your nose and the razor is on your neck." We wanted to survive very badly, to see what would happen to the murderers.

Rumors began to spread that the Russians were already in Vilna and were coming closer to us. We also heard that the partisans were getting stronger and were starting to attack the Germans, coming closer to our camp. On the ninth of July, our camp leader got an order to get the whole camp back to the ghetto. From there they would evacuate us to Germany.

The camp leader guaranteed us that no harm would come to us until we got back to the ghetto. "But what will happen to you in Germany," he said, "I don't know." He told us that no one should try to run away or he would be shot right on the spot. If we heard shots while we were on the road, we should drop to the ground and stay there until told to get up. We were so disappointed and disgusted that we would have to go to Germany that nobody wanted to believe it.

A few friends said to me, "How can you believe them? He is going to take us into the woods and shoot us right there. And if they don't shoot us here, what will happen to us when we get to Germany? They are going to keep us until we die of hunger and cold." Different ideas surfaced everywhere. In spite of the leader's warning, a few of my friends decided that, as soon as they were deep in the woods, they would run to the partisans.

My feeling was different. I had heard that the partisans who were in the woods around us, after we started back to the ghetto, would attack our guards and free the whole camp, and we wouldn't have to suffer any more. But my feeling was unfounded. Most of my friends did run away from the camp, not with the help of the partisans but with the help of the Russian guards.

Here is how it happened. The next morning, about noon, we got an order to line up four abreast. They told us to march to the ghetto, about twenty-five miles. During this march we were guarded by the Germans and the Russians. The road we were marching on was sandy and around us were thick woods. You couldn't see more than five feet into the woods. As we kept walking, it grew dark. As soon as it was fully dark one Russian guard shot into the air. The rest of the guards, hearing the shot, started shooting, too—they thought it was the partisans attacking. With all my friends, I dropped to the ground and crawled on my hands and knees, pulling myself deeper into the woods. I thought the partisans had come and that soon we would all be free.

When the shooting stopped I crawled back out onto the road, thinking that the partisans had taken over the brigade. I felt a sinking feeling in my heart when I heard the German leader shouting to get back into formation. The German guards were running around ready to shoot and yelling to those in the woods to come out. They started shooting into the woods, but they couldn't see anyone; they were just shooting to scare them. The guards didn't want to go any deeper into the woods since they were scared themselves. As we got back together, we saw that all the Ukranian guards and about one hundred people had run away into the woods. There were about three hundred of us left.

What apparently happened is that the guards knew the Red Army was close to Kovno and they wanted to be in good standing with the Russians by helping a few Jews escape from German hands. You can understand the feeling of the rest of us. I had been in the woods. If I had just stayed out there five more minutes I could have been free with the rest, but I had come out and given myself up into the murderers' hands. It bothered me so much that I didn't know what to do with myself.

"On the other hand," I said to myself, "maybe this is God's wish. Maybe this is the better way, who knows?" Later on I heard from friends after the war that a lot of those who ran away were killed in the crossfire between the Germans and the Lithuanians as they ran around in the woods looking for partisans. On Wednesday, July 12, we came back to the ghetto.

25. Deportation to the Concentration Camps

After they brought us into the ghetto, the German leader took us out onto the big field next to the German commandant's headquarters, where I had worked earlier. Already on the field were many Jews from the ghetto or from other working camps outside the ghetto. We had to wait until they had the right number of people for the carloads so they could start deporting us to Germany. Every little while the Germans would bring in moles, people they had found hiding in the ghetto. While we waited, I wandered around to see if I could find my uncles or aunts or anyone who might know what had happened to them.

I asked some friends and neighbors I saw, but they said they hadn't seen them, and that if they were not on the field they might have been deported the day before by barge downriver to the Baltic Sea. I could not be satisfied with that. Were they really taken or were they hiding in the ghetto? I had to escape from the field, even though it was surrounded by German, Lithuanian, and Ukrainian guards, and even though on every other block in the ghetto were German guards tearing up houses and blowing them up with dynamite.

As night came I took the darkness as a cover and escaped from the field to search for my relatives. First I ran to Uncle Abraham's to see what had happened to him. I jumped over fences and crawled on all fours to avoid the searchlights of the Germans. I found myself crawling over dead bodies. I touched their faces with my hands; sometimes I even lifted their heads to see if they were still alive. When I heard guards marching by with flashlights, I got between the bodies and pretended I was dead. As I heard them walk by, I began crawling on all fours again. When I came to the place where my uncle's house had been, there was nothing. Not just his house was gone; the whole block was nothing but rubble. The Germans had blown up the houses to get those hiding in the cellars. I sank to the ground, sobbing quietly. I was near hysterics. Why were we being punished like this? As I began to calm down, I looked about me and lost my will to go on. I didn't want to go look for my other uncles and aunts. If I had stayed there, I might have been able to survive until the Russians came, but I didn't think of that. I went back to the field hoping to find out something about my family.

When I returned to the field, I saw that 90 percent of the people were already gone. Someone told me they had taken a big transport of Jews out already. "Why are the rest of you here?" I asked.

"They just found us. We were hiding in the ghetto."

The next morning the Germans brought in a special demolition squad and bloodhounds. They began to work more quickly. They went back to the same houses they had already torn down and went over them. They didn't trust yesterday's dynamite; they wanted to make sure that everyone was either caught or dead. Each minute they brought in more Jews they had found hiding. Half-naked, half-dead, some of them still had babies in their arms as they came to the field.

We were waiting for orders to march from the ghetto, but some—the old, the sick, the feeble-minded, the cripples and invalids and children—couldn't walk and couldn't be deported. Mr. Goecke ordered that they all be taken to the Jewish hospital and that it be set on fire. He ordered the rest of us to get in lines of four. Germans with machine guns guarded us as we marched; there seemed to be almost a guard for every Jew. They didn't take us through the middle of town but led us through the side streets so fewer people would see us. Some Jews tried to run from the lines to the Lithuanians, and the guards shot them down immediately. Very few succeeded in running away. It began to pour down rain, and when we arrived at the train station we were soaked.

To the Concentration Camps

Forty empty cattle cars were waiting for us. They began separating us into groups of the right number for each car. They pushed us into the cars until we were packed in like herrings. There was no room to sit or lie down. The boxcars were closed and the only air came through a little window in the front that was covered with barbed wire. We hoped the train would start moving soon so we could perhaps get a little air.

As soon as we began moving people started pushing each other, each trying to get a little closer to the window. I saw one young man, around thirty-five, trying to push himself to the window with all his power. As he got close to it, he pulled a pair of wire cutters from his pocket. He cut the wire and, when we had gone only a few kilometers from the station, he pulled himself through the window and jumped from the car. I am not sure if he made it out alive or not, but I don't think he did. Around me was the sound of Jews saying prayers before death.

All of us were tired from standing up so long and sleepy too. There was hardly room to stand. Another man and I turned back to back and put our heads on each other's shoulders. We were pressed so close that the pressure from the bodies of others held us up. This way we fell asleep and slept for several hours. When I woke, I couldn't feel my legs; it was as if they had been amputated. I tried to bend down to give them a massage and I pulled my leg up a little to make sure it was still mine, but as soon as I did, the man standing next to me started yelling, "Hey, why are you kicking me in the back? Put your foot down!" We rode this way for two days and two nights, without food or drink.

Food is food, but the thirst was awful. The worst death is from thirst. Panic started in the boxcar. People started crying to the German guards to give us a little water to drink, but they heard nothing. People began to faint and quite a number died. The guards stopped the train and opened the doors to carry off the bodies of the dead, then closed the doors and started up again. We began to get more and more desperate for water. It got so bad that people began drinking their own urine. I didn't, but those who did found that it burned their throats.

On the third day, we stopped in some kind of station; where, we didn't know. When we stopped, the guards opened the doors to let in a little fresh air. As a guard opened our door, I pulled myself close to him and fell to his feet, begging him to have compassion and give me a little water. It looked like he had a heart in him after all. He took me down from the boxcar and we went up to the locomotive. There was a pipe running from the engine and dirty water was running out. As soon as I saw that water, my eyes opened wide and I pulled off the cap I was wearing and put it under the pipe. I began to pour the water into me as fast as I could, but the water was hot and burned my throat and tongue. I began to drink more slowly. Even though the water was hot and dirty, to me it tasted like heaven. When I was pretty well satisfied, I filled my hat to take back to the boxcar to give a little to some of the others. We were on the train four days and nights altogether.

On July 17, 1944, we arrived at the concentration camp at Auschwitz. They opened the boxcar and told us to run out and get in lines of four. At the same time, they started taking the bodies of the dead from the cars. When we left Kovno there were forty boxcars of Jews, but only fifteen ended up here. The rest were taken to Dachau. There were many Jews who helped unload us. They were wearing striped Sing Sing uniforms with a yellow star of David on the heart and on the back, and each had a number printed on his hand. There were Jews from France, Poland, all over Europe.

Right away the Germans started to sort us out again. They put the ones they thought they could get some work out of in one group and the old and sick in another, the women and children in a third; the half-dead, the very ill, were in a fourth group.

In a photo sent to the uncles in America, Harry Gordon, age three or four, sits on the steps of a government building in Kovno below the statue of the Fallen Lithuanian Soldier. Surrounding him are his father, Yakob Gordon, his mother, Eva Ganckewitz Gordon, his Uncle Abraham Gizelter, and his Aunt Ettel Ganckewitz Gizelter, Eva's oldest sister.

Above left, Abraham and Ettel Gizelter, Harry's guardians after his mother was murdered and his father sent away, in a formal prewar photograph sent to Ettel's brothers in America. Both died during the Holocaust. *Above right,* Uncle Borach Shapiro, husband of Eva's youngest sister, Celia. A salesman dealing in German candy and dishes before the war, he survived Auschwitz and Dachau with Harry. After the war he learned that his son Maishke had survived Buchenwald. *Below,* an early photo of Celia, Solomon, and Golda Ganckewitz, Harry's aunts and uncle, who lived in his grandfather Ganckewitz's apartment house, along with the Gordons. All three died during the Holocaust.

Harry, at about seven or eight, with his Aunt Celia on the balcony of their home in Kovno.

The Ganckewitz sisters—Celia, Golda, Eva, and Ettel (missing from the picture)—were devoted to each other.

Above, the Ninth Fort, where 40,000 executions took place: 25,000 Kovno Jews, 10,000 Jews deported from Germany, Austria, and Czechoslovakia, and thousands of Jewish prisoners of war who had served in the Red Army. Photo by Diane Franzen, 1984. *Below,* the gate to a tunnel in the Ninth Fort, possibly one of the tunnels used in the December 25, 1943, escape. Photo by Diane Franzen, 1984.

A towering monument at the Ninth Fort, built by the Soviet Union in memory of those who died there. An inscription at its base reads "To the Victims of Fascism." Photo by Diane Franzen, 1984.

Above, Harry, second from the right in the first row, at Bad Wörishofen, where he waited for his papers from the U.S. to come through and where he met his wife, Jean (Genya Lelonik), from Poland. *Below,* Harry (left) at a Friday night Shabbas dinner at Bad Wörishofen.

A monument at Bad Wörishofen erected in memory of Jews killed in the Holocaust.

Harry, about twenty-five years old, at Vilas Park in Madison, Wisconsin. The Jewish Welfare Council there arranged jobs for him at the Oscar Mayer plant and later at a dairy. *Below,* the Gordon family on Thanksgiving Day 1962, thankful to be in America and American citizens. Harry and Jean's children are Eric (age eleven), Vivian (one), and Abraham (nine).

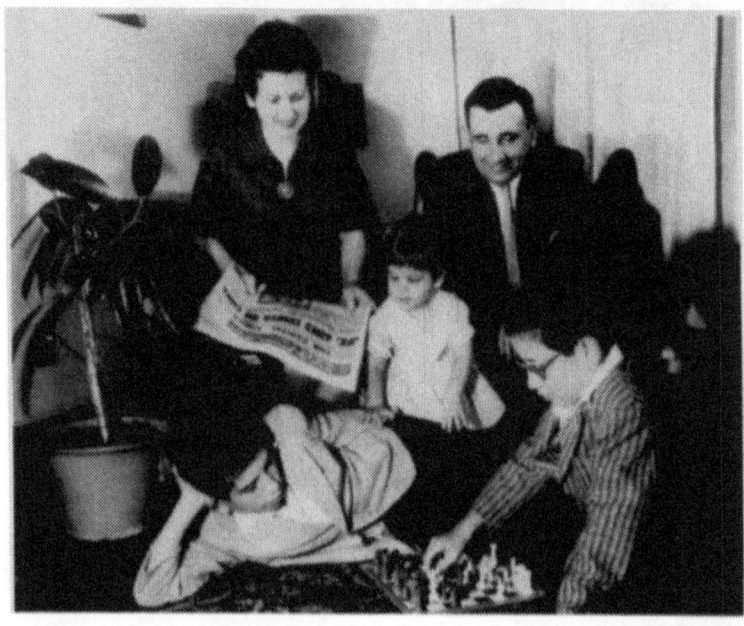

26. Auschwitz

The sorting of the people took between four and five hours. They didn't just consider age; they looked into the face and at the body to see if they could get a little more work out of it. Again, the finger pointed to life or death. A lot of young men fell into the nonworking group. If the Germans didn't like the look on your face or any such thing, you could be put in that group. I fell into the group with the working men.

They took us into the camp to the showers. Over the door was written in German "Delousing." We were each given a towel and sent where we could wash ourselves, then were taken to the delousing showers. As long as we were still working men, they took us into the place where there was real water. We didn't know at that time about the gas chambers.

When the other group, the nonworkers, were told to go into the shower, it was completely different. They were sent to the building right next to us. An electric door shut behind them. When they turned on the water, gas came out. As soon as they were all dead, the floor lowered to the basement, where other Jews were waiting with little wagons to take the bodies to the furnace to be burned.

Before we got into the shower, the Germans took all our clothes and told us to stand in line. Each was searched by the SS for valuables hidden in our teeth or hair. We washed ourselves and thought they would bring our clothes back, but instead everyone got a striped uniform and a pair of shoes with wooden soles and linen tops that laced up to the ankle. The Germans ordered us to get dressed and line up in fours. We did this and started marching to the camp.

On that march what we saw we could hardly believe. The camp was colossal. It seemed to me that all the Jews in the world were there. I also was told that, not far from that camp, there was another camp that held Germans who had said something against Hitler or were criminals before the war. In our camp there were only men. Not far away was a camp where they kept Jewish women. The camps were surrounded by heavy electrified wires. We saw people pushing two-wheeled wheelbarrows; inside the wheelbarrows were live people who looked dead, skeletons covered with skin. One tried to move his hand, another to lift his leg, but they couldn't move. I also saw Jewish police and other Jewish leaders trying to win favor with the Germans by punishing their Jewish brothers.

They took us into a big wooden barracks where there must have been at least a thousand people. I asked them when they had arrived and they told me they had come the day before. There was hardly room to stand, but they told us to sit down. The only way we could sit was for each one to sit between the legs of the one behind him. I began to get acquainted with Jews from all over Europe. I heard many languages: Italian, French, Polish, German. We looked at each other and thought, "Here are more Jews for destruction." We sat this way for a day and a night. We were made to do different kinds of exercises so we would not be able to sleep.

Thank God, we got through that twenty-four hours and they started putting us into groups to go to different barracks. I made friends with another fellow, and we both fell into the same group. Our leader was a Greek who was watching not only our group of one thousand but another group as well. Each of us was taken into a barracks and told where we could sleep. When my friend and I found out where we were assigned, we ran out and looked for water to drink. We found a tap where the water was clean and tasted so good that we didn't want to leave it. We drank all that we could and went back to the barracks to rest on the boards that would be our beds.

As we started to relax, the Greek leader, looking well fed, came into the barracks; he didn't say anything, but he took out the piece of rubber hose he carried and beat us with it. We escaped with our lives and later learned from the older citizens that no one could be in the barracks between 5:00 AM and 9:00 PM. As we talked we could see the fire from the furnace in full swing. The veterans told us that the fire never went out but burned night and day. Music was played throughout the whole camp so we wouldn't hear the screams of the innocent victims. It could be heard for miles. We couldn't wait until nine o'clock so we could go to sleep.

Finally we went in and fell onto the hard boards on the ground. At ten the gas lamps had to be out. As soon as the light was out, despite the crowd of people, I fell asleep. My sleep didn't last long. At 2:00 AM screaming and crying began and I jumped up. They were yelling in German that everyone should get out of the barracks and be ready to be counted. My friend and I, half-asleep weren't used to the rules of the concentration camp; we dressed a little more slowly than the rest of the group. We thought we had time. Right away the Greek leader came over and let us have it. Quickly we learned the new orders. We ran out for the counting and stood in line for three hours. At five they split us into groups and took us to work. We mixed cement, carried bricks, and pushed wheelbarrows loaded with sand.

I was put in the working brigade that helped unload the boxcars. There were Jews arriving from all over Europe. As when we arrived, the first thing the Germans did was catch the children and throw them into trucks like sacks of potatoes. Not far from the camp were large pits. The truck, a dump truck, would back up to the hole and dump the children out like a load of gravel. They would shoot them, then spray them with gasoline and set fire to them.

At the same time, they sorted the working from the nonworking men. One group went to the showers, the other to the gas chambers. The screaming and crying would tear your heart apart. I decided, after a few days of this job, that I couldn't take any more of the pain and sorrow of my brothers and sisters.

Each night when we came back from work, our leader, the Greek, would hand us a ration of bread, two pounds for ten people, and a quart of soup each. They called it vegetable soup, but really it was water. If in the whole quart of soup I found one bean or slice of carrot, it was a big event.

The next morning I started on a different brigade. I didn't

know it, but this brigade would be a thousand times worse than the one I was on before. In this one I played with my life. I saw that each morning the Germans caught people for some kind of working brigade, so I, a stupid fool, volunteered. It looked like I was the only volunteer; the rest they had to catch. We started out a couple of hundred, but when we came back we were less than half. We had to push a large wheelbarrow filled with cement, but not at a walk; we had to run with it. Those who couldn't run were shot by the Germans. For them it was a big game. They were laughing and having a big time of it. The partner I was pushing a wheelbarrow with let go of his handle, and as he did so the guard shot him right away. When I came back to camp, I thought that I had come back from the dead. I promised myself they would not find me in that brigade as a volunteer again. I would never volunteer for anything but would just wait for my luck. Where the Germans told me to go, I would go, but I was not going to volunteer.

Every day the ration of bread got smaller and smaller. The situation grew steadily worse and our hunger got stronger. I could see that nobody would escape alive from that camp. A few of my friends thought the same thing and decided to volunteer to go to the hospital. I told them that if they gave themselves up to the hospital, they would not see the light of day again, because we knew what the Germans did to the sick. But they told me they couldn't take it any more; they didn't want to keep suffering and we didn't know how long it would be until the war was over. They would probably kill us anyway. They gave themselves up and I didn't see them again. Listening to the stories and seeing what was going on in this camp, I thought I would never get out alive.

27. Dachau, Camp Number One

In the beginning of September 1944, I was deported with a group of people to Dachau. It was also surrounded with a high electrified fence, but the barracks weren't as big as at Auschwitz. These barracks had fewer people, fifty to seventy-five, but they were excavated into the ground. Each had one little window, and the only one allowed to stay by this window was the leader of that particular barracks. Our camp was men only; the women were held in a camp across from us. Most of the people in this camp were survivors from the Kovno ghetto.

When I heard that most of the Jews were from Kovno, I became excited, hoping that perhaps I would meet my uncles and maybe find out where my aunts were and what had happened to them. They might even be in the women's camp across the way. When I went to the barracks where I had been assigned, I met a lot of people I knew from the ghetto. The leader of my barracks was a Jewish policeman from the ghetto.

The next morning as we were standing in line to be counted and told what kind of working brigades we would be assigned to, suddenly I saw two familiar faces quite a distance away—Uncle Borach and my father! I couldn't believe they were there. I had not seen my father for three years. I had thought for sure that he was dead, and he thought that I was dead too. Here we were, two dead ones brought back together alive. We ran to each other. We started hugging and kissing each other in happiness, all three crying like babies. Each began telling his story of how he got to the camp. My father had been in several different camps. Uncle Borach had been brought here by boat after the ghetto was blown up. They were both drawn and thin but didn't look too bad. My uncle was hoping that Aunt Celia and Maishke were still alive, and I began to hope too. I couldn't believe that I had found my uncle and father! We had to stop our conversation when the orders came to march to work.

While we worked on the roads and in the field building a hangar, hauling bricks and cement, we kept talking to each other when we could. The hangars we were building were made of cement and iron and were fortified so that bombs wouldn't be able to destroy the planes inside. For this job they brought in German master builders who belonged to what was called the Organization of Death. They wore brown uniforms, black boots, and a white band on the arm, marked with two letters: AD. This hangar we were working on was very large and was being built in the middle of the woods for camouflage from the English and American planes.

We stopped work at six in the evening. The Germans told us to line up in fours to march back to camp. As we walked, we carried the bodies of the dead back on planks; some had died from beatings, some from hunger. Here they did not burn the bodies but buried them in a common grave. When we got back to camp we got our rations—a two pound loaf of bread for ten people and a quart of soup each. After I got my rations, I very quietly went to my father's barracks. I wanted to find out what had happened to the rest of my uncles and aunts. Uncle Borach, who was in the same barracks as my father, told me that he didn't know anything about Uncle Abraham, Uncle Yenchik and his family, or even about Aunt Celia and Maishke, since they were taken away from him before he came to this camp. I went back to my barracks to sleep.

At 1:00 in the morning, I heard the Germans call us to line up for counting. Each night they would awaken us at a different time, startling us out of our sleep just to punish us. I got dressed quickly and ran out to stand in a line of four. We stood in line until five o'clock, when they told us to go to work. By the time they told us to march, we were glad to move because we were cold and marching warmed us a little. My feet were already numb from standing in the cold, but when we started moving, I

Dachau, Camp Number One

could feel my legs again. We had to walk about six miles to work. Every day I could see more and more people dying from hunger and pain from beatings. Some of the master builders were in their fifties and sixties, and they weren't too bad, but the younger Germans would kick and hit us while we worked.

My particular master, a German engineer, used to bring me food that he had left over from his rations. The extra soup and bread helped me a lot, but it didn't last long. The Germans brought in a different master who would beat the hell out of us.

Every day as we came back to camp we were one day closer to liberation, but the hunger worked on us stronger and stronger. From hour to hour, each of us was getting weaker. Within a day a person seemed to age ten years.

One morning, about three days after I arrived, I saw the German commandant from the camp was going between the lines with a couple of SS men as we were being counted. They were looking into the faces of the older ones to see who would not last much longer and were pulling these people from the lines. They pulled out about a hundred people. My father was in that group. They put them on trucks and took them away. From that day on I never saw my father. There were some rumors that they took that particular group to the crematorium at Auschwitz. You can understand how I felt in my heart. After such a long separation to be together again and to know that liberation was not far off—and then he had to die.

That same night we heard air raid sirens. American and English planes came over the little town nearby to bombard it. All the Germans in the camp, including the German commandant, ran to the bomb shelters we had built to hide themselves. But as we heard the sirens, we ran out into the field and stood near the barracks, watching with happiness. It was like revenge, and we danced for joy. This bombardment went on for several days.

When they bombarded during the day, while we were at work, the master builders and guards would run to hide, but we would stay in the middle of the field, loving it. We prayed that they would keep bombarding so that we would not have to work, but, as soon as the planes left, the guards and masters would come back and, knowing that we were happy about the raid, take it out on us.

Winter came and nature wasn't good to us, either. We had to contend with hunger, cold, dirt, lice, and the Germans. The lice drank the little blood we had left. The hunger became worse, and people started catching little animals, whatever they could find, even cats and dogs. Even though the hunger was punishing me, I couldn't take seeing people catching the animals, even rats. I felt that my end was coming closer.

My shoes tore apart and I couldn't get any others. I had to walk barefoot to work in the twenty-degree weather. As I walked from camp to work, I found cement bags and wrapped my feet in them, but they were only paper and as I walked over the rough terrain they tore off. I could tell that my feet were freezing and I kept trying to find new sacks. When the German guards saw me doing this as I worked, they would beat me. I got so depressed at this time that I thought my whole life wasn't worth anything. I was jealous of the dead ones. I lost all my hope.

One clear, cold morning when we reached the field to go to work, I ran up to a German guard and said to him, "Why don't you shoot me?"

He looked at me and said, "This bullet is worth more than you are. Why should I shoot you? You are going to die anyway."

Not far from us there was a German master builder standing who heard me talking to the guard. He called me over and asked me, "Why do you want that guy to shoot you?"

"I don't have anything to lose," I said to him. "I walk around hungry, naked; my feet are frozen. I would be better off dead."

He didn't answer me. He pulled me into a little tool shed and took from a box a new pair of wooden shoes. He told me to put them on and at the same time gave me a canteen full of soup and told me to eat it. As I put on the shoes and ate the soup, I began to hope again, to think that perhaps I would live. For me, this was a miracle from God, a pair of shoes, some hot soup, and a chance to get warmed.

When I came back to camp that night and told Uncle Borach what had happened to me, he couldn't believe it, but when I showed him my new shoes he had to believe. Even with the

Dachau, Camp Number One

shoes, I felt that I was still getting weaker by the hour. I felt that what I had gone through until now I wouldn't be able to survive again. I started eating cat meat, whatever I could find.

Rumors spread that the Germans were going to take volunteers who wanted to go to a sick camp. These people wouldn't have to work anymore and could stay there until they died. When I heard the news I ran to my uncle. We decided that, no matter what would happen, good or bad, we would volunteer for the sick camp. In the next day or two, when we were standing in line to be counted, the commandant gave an order that the sick and old people would be taken to the sick camp. My uncle and I volunteered with a hundred or so other people. Even with this many volunteers, the commandant still went between the lines to pull out people. Many people were afraid that they would be shot or burned or gassed. We knew what a German sick camp could mean. But to our amazement our whole group was taken to camp number four at Dachau.

28. The Sick Camp

We were moved to Camp Number Four at the end of January 1945 on a cold, overcast day. The commandant gave the order for us to march to the new camp, which was about twenty miles. The road was very bad and covered with snow. People started falling from hunger and cold. Uncle Borach and I tried to pick some up, but they were too heavy for us to drag. They couldn't get up, so the guards shot them. Many people froze their hands and feet. My uncle and I, half-dead, made it to the camp.

At the camp they gave us a ration of a two-pound loaf of bread for twenty people and a quart of soup; then they told us what barracks we belonged to. In the barracks were Jews of different nationalities—Russians, Poles. The dirt was unbelievable. Each barracks held seventy-five to a hundred people. We looked bad, but the people who had been there for a while looked worse. We called them skeletons.

When we finished our rations, we all crowded around the little stove in the middle of the barracks, all one hundred of us, trying to get close to the fire to delouse ourselves. You could hear the lice popping from the heat. The cracking of the lice sounded like an orchestra. As long as we kept our Sing Sing jackets off and were close to the fire, they didn't eat us so much, but as soon as we moved away from the fire and put our jackets on, it was not five minutes until we could pull them from our underarms by the bunch.

I started making friends, asking people where they came from and telling them about myself. We all asked each other, "Did you bump into so-and-so? Did you see that person?" I asked

The Sick Camp

about the sick camp, about what we did here. One fellow told me that, even in the sick camp, there were working brigades. One took dead bodies from the camp, a second took garbage from the kitchen, and a third went to work building hangars. But all these brigades were made up of volunteers, the strongest. The rest sat in camp and waited for the big miracle.

The next morning I went to Uncle Borach and suggested that we go from barracks to barracks to look for someone from our family. We started looking and, to our amazement, met Uncle Yenchik. Our happiness is impossible to describe. One didn't want to let the other talk; each wanted to be the first to tell all that had happened to him. Uncle Yenchik told us how he was taken from the ghetto. Aunt Golda and the children were hiding with him in the cellar, but when he heard the Germans blowing up the houses and setting fire to them, he volunteered for the deportation. After they arrived in the town of Stuthoff, the Germans took Aunt Golda and the children and sent Uncle Yenchik to the sick camp. He was very pale and moved slowly, this man who had been as strong as two horses. He said that he wished he had stayed in the hiding place in the ghetto. If they had to die, at least they would all have died together. "Right now," he said, "this is not death or life." We tried to encourage him, telling him that with the help of God, we would be left alive and maybe the rest of the family would be too. We had to hope for the best. As our conversation ended, we asked each other, "Maybe you have a little food left over from yesterday?" Nobody had anything left, not even from today.

I said to my uncles, "Why don't we go to the garbage bin and see if we can find something?" We went to the kitchen and jumped into the large bins, searching with our hands for food like regular pigs. I found a few rotten potatoes and some potato skins and some bones. We took them back to the barracks and washed the food in the washroom. I cut all the rotten stuff from the potatoes with a spoon that I had sharpened on one edge. As we ate, our hunger eased a little.

Every day the ration of bread got smaller and smaller. The slices of bread we got were so moldy that it looked like smoke was coming out. Even then, we would watch it and eat slowly so it would last longer, and if a little piece of mold fell onto the ground, we would pick it up and eat it, eating a little piece of dirt with it. I would sit down on the ground in the barracks and with the sharp edge of my spoon cut the bread into little pieces, as if I were feeding a bird, because then it would last longer. I would think that I should leave half a piece for tomorrow morning, so I would put half a slice in my jacket and put it under my head to sleep, but I knew that half slice of bread was there and it bothered me. I was hungry, why shouldn't I eat it then? Let God worry about tomorrow.

I was so hungry that I used to think that, if I survived, I would get in a big room full of bread and sit in the middle and eat all I wanted. I didn't think of furniture or houses or cars, just bread. There were some people who would give away a half slice of bread for half a cigarette or a little snuff. It was hard for me to believe, to give away bread for a bit of smoke. One man asked me for a cigarette for his slice of bread. I told him I couldn't give him a cigarette, I didn't have any, and he fell dead right there in front of me. Many of those who wanted cigarettes were Russians. They would tear leaves from trees and roll cigarettes from them.

Many people would save a half slice of bread for the next day. A lot of times, in the middle of the night, I would feel hands crawling all over me, trying to steal some bread. People knew that five minutes later they might be dead anyway. Sometimes someone would catch hold of the hands or catch a leg. A big hullabaloo would start, with people yelling, "Thief! Give me back my bread." There would be cursing and screaming, and the whole barracks would wake up. The leader, who slept by the stove, didn't know who to catch or which way to go. It would last for a half hour and then things would quiet down.

One night as I was sleeping, I could feel hands crawling over me and my jacket. I let them look, since I had no bread hidden and all they could find on me was lice. But they didn't let go, and the long fingernails started scratching my face. Slowly I took off my shoe, which I slept in so no one would steal it, and I hit one of the hands with the wooden sole. The person started screaming, "He is killing me! He is killing me!" and ran. From that night on, no one bothered me again.

The Sick Camp

In this camp, we were not human any more, we were parasites living on each other's blood. Each waited for the other to die so he could take his little piece of bread or his jacket or shoes. Each wanted to save himself by his friend's death. Dead bodies were lying around in the barracks, so an epidemic started—typhus or cholera, I'm not sure what it was.

As soon as the Germans heard that the camp had an epidemic, they closed us off. They wouldn't let anyone in or out. In one week, the epidemic took over the whole camp. I was the only one in our barracks who was sitting with the sick ones; all the rest of the camp was sick. The only medicine we had was cold water. There were no doctors. I gave everyone cold water and put cold compresses on their heads, since with this sickness came a very high fever. People became delirious; they ran back and forth. One yelled, "Let me out! My train is standing waiting for me! I have to get home!" Another said, "Get away from me! I will kill you! I will stab you with my knife!"

Such sick ones I took care of. Hundreds died from the sickness. It is hard to describe how their bodies looked; they were completely rotted. It was as if their skin rotted away and left big holes.

I was the last one in the barracks to get the disease. I had no one to bring me water or cold compresses. I felt my fever growing. For a few days I lost my senses. But, as the saying goes, "If you have to stay alive, you stay alive." The one good thing about the sickness was that it made me forget my hunger pains. I lay on the ground for fourteen days until the crisis passed. I knew when I felt the pain of hunger that my sickness was ending. How I overcame it, I don't know. It was a miracle. Half the camp died.

When I began to feel hunger, I pulled myself together and dragged myself to the door of the barracks, but I couldn't quite make it. I was so weak, my legs moved like those of an eighty-year-old man. I pulled myself back to the place where I had been before and rested. The second day my hunger began to punish me more and more. I had to get my rations. On all fours I began pulling myself toward the barracks door. In order to get out I had to go up three steps. I wanted to get out and get some fresh air and go to the garbage bin to try to find food. As I tried to get up the stairs, I began seeing different colored birds in front of my eyes, and my legs began shaking. With all my strength, I pushed against the door, falling down as it opened. I couldn't stand up on my own, so I crawled near the wall of the barracks and sat up, leaning against it. I couldn't stand the hunger.

Nearby I saw some green grass, so I crawled up to it and tore some off to eat. I pushed it into my mouth like a cow until I felt that my belly was full. I was still hungry, but the grass helped a little bit, and I was able to get up and look through the barracks for Uncle Borach and Uncle Yenchik. We had all survived and, holding onto each other for support, we went to the garbage bin to look for something to eat, potato skins or anything.

There was nothing left; other people had already gone through the bin. With our heads hanging, we started back toward the barracks. As we went, we saw two Russians who had smuggled themselves into the area where the dead bodies were. They were moving them back and forth. Then we saw them throw down two bodies and start cutting off the buttocks with their sharpened spoons. They threw the meat onto a fire they had made. After a while we could see that they were eating it. Even with hunger punishing us so badly, seeing that made us sick.

After the epidemic things became worse because we were all weaker. Green grass became a delicacy, and soon there was no more grass in the camp. Since there was grass growing outside the camp, I put myself in the working brigade that took the dead bodies out of the camp. As soon as I got out of the camp, I started tearing off grass and filling my pockets and a sack I had found. That would be enough grass for me until the next day when I went to work.

29. Liberation

After the epidemic, the hunger became so fierce that, no matter how much grass I put in myself, hunger still cut my soul. The ration of bread was now two pounds of bread for fifty people, and there was no soup. During the last month before the liberation the Germans didn't give us any bread at all, only a quart of water each.

The bombardments by the American and English planes were daily occurrences. The planes would fly in and circle around our camp with white smoke, marking the camp so they wouldn't bombard that area. They must have known exactly where all the camps in Germany were, because later on I heard that other camps were marked with smoke too. As soon as the Americans and English began bombing the large German cities, the Germans didn't even put up a fight. All they did was set off alarms to tell the people to go into hiding, and sometimes even the alarms came too late. We could tell that all was chaos. The German machine wasn't working as it had in the beginning. Deliverance was not far away.

But the question was, what would happen to us? Every day our German camp commander would tell us, "You stinking Jews, if Germany loses the war you won't be left alive anyway. Even if Germany capitulates at twelve noon, you will all be killed at five minutes before twelve." They would have done it if they had had the time. The last order given by Himmler, at the end of March 1945, was to kill every human being, every Jew, left in the concentration camps. Thank God, because of the rush of the American and English offensive, the German murderers didn't have enough time to finish his last order, or there would have been no witnesses. But they had everything ready to do it.

The liquidation of all the concentration camp inmates was to be done in the German Alps, where supposedly they had ready machine guns manned by German soldiers waiting for their victims. They waited in vain. An order was given on April 26, 1945, to evacuate our camp.

The Germans told us all to get ready and stand in lines of four to march to the train, which was about fifteen miles away. Those who could, walked; the others were put in wheelbarrows or little wagons and were pulled by the healthier ones. I tried to stay with my two uncles. The march to the train was hard. Every one of us knew that this was our last march, that we were taking our last steps. We knew we were going to be killed. Many people fell on the road as we marched; those who couldn't get up were shot. We knew they were going to kill us, but each of us who could still walk hoped that a miracle would happen and we would be left alive.

What pushed us to keep moving and keep hoping? Revenge! We wanted to see what would happen to the murderers. It was only a question of days now. We could tell by the way the Germans pushed everything faster and faster.

Everyone who had a little strength moved toward the front of the lines, because those who fell behind would be shot. Uncle Yenchik started complaining that he couldn't walk any more, and he began to fall back, but Uncle Borach and I wouldn't let him go. We put our shoulders under his arms and tried to help him. We were both so weak we could hardly move ourselves, but from somewhere the power came and we didn't just drag him, we lifted him from the ground and took him forward. As we kept moving, the load got heavier and heavier and all three of us began to drop back. Uncle Yenchik could see this and told us to let him go so we could get in the front of the lines. But we wouldn't let him go. We pulled him until we got close to the station, when we got a wheelbarrow from someone who had died and put him in that.

When we came to the station there was a line of boxcars in which they had hauled coal, open boxcars, waiting for us. The

Liberation

Germans divided us up so many to a car; Uncle Borach and I got into the same one, while Uncle Yenchik was put in a different one with a lot of sick people. We never saw him again. As I understand it, he was killed on the train.

The engine started pulling us slowly. After a couple of hours we had to stop in a station for the night. We couldn't get by because the German military trains were going through, running from the front lines. Many tracks were bombarded and ruined also; that is why our train went so slowly. We stopped about fifteen miles past Landsberg on April 27, 1945, a beautiful sunny morning. We heard over our heads the heavy roar of airplane engines. The German guards jumped down from the boxcars and hid themselves in the woods by the tracks, keeping their rifles pointed at us so we wouldn't run. We could see the planes coming closer and closer, flying very low over us. They opened fire with machine guns. The first shots were at the engines and the two boxcars behind it. Several hundred people were killed, torn open by the firing. The pilots thought we were German troops. A few hours later more planes came down and fired on us, but we had taken a couple of boards from the boxcar and put some of our Sing Sing jackets on them, and we waved them in the air. They were flying low and must have seen them and understood that we were concentration camp prisoners because they flew away and didn't come back.

Later in the afternoon we could see guards running from several boxcars that were on fire. We didn't know what was going on, so we jumped from our boxcars and hid in the forest. My uncle and I saw several prisoners running with boxes of cookies and even socks, so we asked them where they got those things. It was the two cars that held the German guards' rations that were on fire. We saw as we neared the cars that prisoners were pushing themselves in through the fire and were yelling. Uncle Borach and I ran up and went in ourselves and got two packages of cookies and two pairs of women's nylons.

This didn't last long because not all the guards had run away. There were still a few who believed in the Führer, and they started shooting at us to get us back together and into the boxcars. Even though everything was chaos, the machine to exterminate us was still working. We could see the smoke from towns burning a few miles away, the engine on the train was out of commission, and three-quarters of the guards had deserted, but still the Germans pulled up another engine and took all the people they could catch farther on toward the German Alps. But they only made it for another fifteen miles before they were stopped again and the prisoners were liberated.

Uncle Borach and I had decided to escape. We ran across an open field, the German guards shooting over our heads. It began to pour rain and we kept running, holding onto each other, not even looking back to see if anyone was running after us. We didn't know where we were going; we were driven. It began to get dark and I felt my feet sinking into the ground as it rained harder. I had a hard time pulling my legs out of the mud as I ran, so I told Uncle Borach, "Let's walk a little slower. I don't have any more strength."

As we walked, Uncle Borach thought he saw a barn a little way off. When we got to it, we went in to look for some hay. There was no light and we didn't want to make much noise and arouse any farm dogs. We were afraid we would be found by the owner and shot. We felt around like blind men until we found a rail and some steps and followed them to a pile of hay. We crawled underneath and thought this would be our best hiding place until the Americans showed up. We were soaked to the skin and shaking like leaves.

My uncle was worried that German soldiers would find us and shoot us on the spot. I said, "Hey, they have enough problems of their own. They aren't going to look for Jews now. We're as good as liberated. Can you imagine, we're going to sit down to a table with a whole loaf of bread, with butter, and we'll be able to eat as much as we want."

I could tell his mouth was watering. He couldn't believe we were already free men. We had forgotten what being free was all about. He couldn't even comprehend it. With these thoughts in our minds, we fell asleep and didn't wake until about six in the morning, when we heard voices downstairs.

The voices sounded just like German soldiers, and we heard heavy machinery starting up. Then someone was coming up the

Liberation

steps and throwing hay from our hiding spot. He pulled up a fork of hay and there we were. We were lucky not to get forked. The man looked at me, frozen. He didn't know what to do. He called downstairs to the others to come up. The three men were prisoners of war, two Frenchmen and a Pole, who were working on a German farm. They asked us how we had gotten there, and we told them the whole story. They told us that the Americans were quite a ways off but they should be coming in about five days. On Sunday the Americans would be in Landsberg, and they would take us there. In the meantime they would find a better hiding place for us so the German boss wouldn't find us. They picked us up, we were so thin, and carried us over to another corner and put some hay over us.

I told the Pole that we were hungry, dead hungry, and before long he brought us a big jug of fresh milk right from the cow and a big loaf of bread. I hadn't seen milk for years. We started tearing off chunks of bread and drinking the milk. There are no words to describe the taste of that meal. But right after I ate, I got diarrhea. A couple of hours later they brought us baked potatoes and more milk, as much as we could eat. Uncle Borach held out pretty well, but I didn't. The Frenchmen kept bringing us food, more than we should have eaten. I put it in one end, but it ran out the other. I didn't care; all I cared about was the food was coming in. We stayed in the barn like this for two days and nights. At 6:00 AM on Sunday, April 29, one Frenchman came in and told us the Americans were in Landsberg, about six miles away. My uncle and I got up and left the barn to walk into the yard. On the porch of the house were the German farmer and his wife observing us. I had a terrible stomach ache and was holding my pants with one hand so they wouldn't fall down, I was so skinny. We were both skin and bones. The farmer called to us, so we went up and his wife brought out old work overalls and a glass of cocoa for each of us, but they wouldn't give us a ride into town. We thanked them and started walking toward Landsberg. My pain was so great that I couldn't keep myself on my feet. My uncle saw how I was suffering and he helped me.

30. In the Hospital

Even with my uncle's help, I had to stop every five steps to catch my breath. On the one hand, I felt the pain in my stomach, but on the other hand, I felt great happiness that we were now free. Tears flowed from our eyes, and our hopes were so high as we reached Landsberg that we thought we would find our families and loved ones who had also been liberated from the murderers.

In the streets were American soldiers with helmets and rifles and tanks, but there were no Germans. The only other people in the streets were the liberated prisoners, the displaced persons. A lot of DPs were already dressed in civilian clothes with their two yellow stars on the front. Others were in their Sing Sing uniforms. My uncle wanted to look for members of our family, but I asked him to help me find a doctor first; I couldn't stand the pain any more. He went to look for a doctor while I sat waiting on the street.

To our luck, he found a Jewish doctor named Dr. Greenburg and asked him where there was a hospital. He told him that there was no hospital yet, but that the Americans were cleaning up a German hospital for the sick DPs. In the meantime, I was to go to a cellar where the sick were waiting. When I got there, there were a lot of people already lying on the ground. Some were slightly sick, some very sick, some couldn't move. I told my uncle to lie down next to me so we could go the the hospital together, but he said he was feeling fine. He left to see if he could find out anything about the rest of the family and to help with the other sick people.

In the cellar, the man next to me said, "Is it true? Are we really free?"

In the Hospital

"Sure," I answered. "We are already a free people. The Americans freed us. We don't have to be afraid of the murderers any more. We don't have to go hungry. We are going to have as much as we want to eat." He started laughing and crying hysterically.

At four in the afternoon American ambulances began arriving, and we were loaded into them. The very sick ones, like me, who couldn't move, were taken on stretchers. Each ambulance took six people. As I was loaded in, I said goodby to my uncle and told him to come see me in the hospital. We were stopped several times on the road by MPs who were controlling the roads. They opened the back to see who was inside. When they looked at our faces, they gave us their knapsacks, whatever they had—food, cigarettes, the whole thing—and they took pictures. By the time we got to the hospital, I had cartons of cigarettes, a few cans of conserves, a lot of chocolate bars, and many other good things.

At the hospital, they opened the doors and Germans with stretchers carried us into the building. They took me up to the shower room. Two Germans took off my Sing Sing clothes and put me, on the stretcher, into the shower to be washed. In the shower were two more German prisoners and two Americans with guns. The Germans were scared that if they didn't do a good job washing me, they would be shot. You can imagine how I felt, after all those years of being under the Germans, to see them washing me while the Americans watched, standing there as prisoners of war, washing the "dirty Jews." It was revenge.

When I was washed, they took me on the stretcher into a room with a scale. They put me on it and I could see that I weighed about fifty pounds. I was feeling pretty cocky by now and I said, "That can't be right. Put me on a different scale."

They said to me in German, "That is a true scale and that is what you weigh." I was just skin and bones. They put me in a fresh gown and took me to a room where there were already about fifty DPs in beds. They put me on an iron bed with a nice soft mattress and fresh white bedding. An hour later two German nuns who were our nurses brought in two kettles of cereal for the people in the room. When the men saw those kettles, those who could jumped from their beds and ran to them and started eating from the ladle. Everyone wanted to be first. The two nuns screamed and ran for the door, running for their lives.

In a little while they came back with two American soldiers with rifles, but by then the kettles were already empty.

The nuns came back with another kettle and were accompanied by the soldiers, so no one jumped out of bed. Each of us was served a little bowl of oatmeal. I was served in bed because I couldn't move. As we finished eating, an American doctor came in and began examining us. I must have looked sicker than any of the others in the room because he came to my bed first. The rest of the patients in this ward were taken care of by German doctors under American supervision, but I was taken care of by the American doctor personally. As soon as he sat down by me, the doctor began giving me shots.

The first month in the hospital was the roughest. One doctor would come in and leave, then another would come in to see me. Many people didn't follow doctor's orders. They tried to eat like pigs right away, and many of them died. Since I couldn't feed myself, my food was regulated; I had to be fed like a little baby. I tried to keep track of the number of shots I was given each day, but I lost count; it was somewhere between twenty and thirty shots.

One evening the American chief surgeon came into the ward and spoke to us. He said, "Jews, try to hold together. Just eat as much as your doctor tells you to eat. You don't have to be scared. You aren't in the concentration camp now. You are free people and you are in the American zone under American supervision. You don't have to worry. There is plenty of food, but right now you cannot eat too much. You are going through the crisis right now between life and death. The other doctors and I are trying our damnedest to make you well, if you will only follow our instructions. We will try to get you in touch with your family and will try to reunite you." He talked in such a nice way and with such a sweet voice, like a mother talking to her children.

American reporters also came in and sat by our beds and asked us what we had been through and took notes, but they didn't come to me. The doctors must have told them that I was too weak to tell them any stories. At the same time, different DPs would come in looking for friends and family. I saw one old Lithuanian Jew come in, and asked him to find out where my

In the Hospital

uncle was. In a couple of days he came back and told me that Uncle Borach was in the same hospital as me, but he was very sick. The friend didn't know what the sickness was. Later I learned that he had a mental breakdown from which he never really recovered.

After six months of hard work by the American doctors, I started sitting up in bed and gaining weight. I began walking around a little with the help of two nuns, but I was a long way from being healthy. I spent two years in that hospital. During this time a lot of DPs had gotten in touch with friends and relatives in the United States and had asked them to send papers for them to go to America. I couldn't even get out of bed to go make any inquiries. A Jewish fellow came in, a Frenchman, from the Joint Distribution Committee, and took names of people who had friends or relatives in the United States. He told us that our names would appear in papers in America in Yiddish and English. He said that he was sure our family there would try to get in touch with us. Since I had three uncles who had gone to America before I was born, my name went on the list, too.

I left the hospital. My first civilian suit was a jacket I got from friends and pants made by a German tailor from an American bedspread. I was taken directly from the hospital to a DP camp. It was a hotel at Bad Wörishofen, where we got our rations from the Americans. We had our own keepers, but had no work to do. We were all waiting for our papers to come through, as were DPs in camps all over Germany. A Jewish committee with headquarters in Munich worked to get our papers in order and try to locate family and friends, but their work was hard; there was no mail or regular communication system.

31. The DP Camp

As soon as I moved to the DP camp, I went every day by train to Munich to the Jewish Committee's office. Every time I went in there would be a new list telling who was still alive and where they were and who was looking for whom. I hoped to find somebody from my family. There would be long lines of people at the offices waiting to hear some news of their families. To our despair, 99 percent of those who waited each day went away disappointed. In spite of this, I didn't give up hope. Every day I wrote letters to Kovno addressed to my family, hoping that someone was left there. Maybe someone had been liberated in the Russian zone and had gone back there. I waited every day for news, but I never got any answers to those letters, to this day.

At this time I was able to get in contact with Uncle Borach, and we got caught up on what had happened. It was two more years before he found out that his son, Maishke, had been liberated at Buchenwald. It took me some time to admit that the three of us were all that was left of our family. My mother and father, Aunt Ettel and Uncle Abraham, Aunt Golda and Uncle Yenchik and their two children, Aunt Celia, and Uncle Shloime—all were gone. At least I had visited Aunt Ettel's grave.

In my particular DP camp there were about a hundred Jews, all survivors of concentration camps. Most were young, about my age. Every two people had a nice room complete with maid service. In the camp were Jews from Lithuania, Poland, Czechoslovakia, and many other countries. In the hotel German cooks prepared food for us. Every month we got a special package from the Joint Distribution Committee which would have in it different kinds of food and clothing. We also developed a training school for the younger DPs, like me, where we could learn a trade so that when we left Germany we would be able to earn a living. Those who went to the school went from three to four hours a day. After school we could get involved in sports. No one wanted to think about going to work for a German industry, to help rebuild the murderers' country. Even if we had, much of the industry and many towns had been leveled by the bombardments. Everyone was thinking of just one thing—emigration.

Everyone wanted to emigrate to the United States, but at this time things were moving very slowly, even for people who already had their papers, because of the quota system. It might take years of waiting. Many got tired of this waiting and voluntarily went to Israel. I had had enough of fighting to survive and couldn't imagine going to Israel and fighting the Arabs. Some DPs were lonely and began marrying German girls and making businesses in Germany. When emigration opened up to Canada, many went there hoping to get into the United States later. I myself wanted to go only to the United States, no matter how long it took.

The Frenchman must have put my name in the American papers in New York, because one day my aunt was reading the paper and noticed that someone was looking for anyone by the name of Ganckewitz. She knew that that had been my uncle's name before he changed it to Ginsberg, so she told him and he told the other uncles, and Uncle Jack got in touch with me and sent the papers I needed. At this time I was lonely, too, and had gotten acquainted with a Polish girl named Genya (Jean) Lalonich in the DP camp. She had been liberated by the Russians but had run away to the American zone after the liberation. Her parents had paid a Polish farmer a great sum of money to hide her during the war. She didn't know Yiddish when she came to Germany, only Polish. Her family had been murdered by the Germans. We had fallen in love, so I wrote to my uncle and asked him to try to make out the papers for myself and my wife, so we could both go to the United States. Before we left we would get married. My uncle wasn't too happy about it, but he had the papers made up as I asked. Now all we had to do was wait until the quota let us in.

The American Congress and President Truman introduced a

new law that would allow an extra 200,000 DPs in above the quota. People were being called to the American Consulate and told to bring all kinds of papers proving they were really DPs and had been in a camp. They were interrogated by the FBI to determine if they were Communists. I got our papers ready for when we would be called.

I would go every day to the Jewish Committee in Munich to get different papers and documents proving that I was Hersh Gordon, born in Kovno, Lithuania. I had to have witnesses that I was who I was. I got in touch with the office in Dachau and got proof that I had been there, an identification with my picture on it, documented by the American commander. Thanks to that document, my emigration proceeded more quickly. Genya and I got married in a religious ceremony, but it was also necessary to have the proper license to show that we were married. The religious documents I got from a Hungarian rabbi, but when I went to get the legal license, I ran into trouble. My wife was only sixteen, so she had to have parental permission. Her parents were dead, so we had to write to the Polish city where she was born to try to find her next of kin. In the meantime, we couldn't legally marry. It might have taken months to find out if she had any relatives left or, if she did not, to get the court to give us permission to marry.

At the same time, the American Consulate wanted all my papers. I didn't know what to do. It wasn't just that she couldn't go to the United States. I couldn't either. Every morning I got up at 4:00 AM and ran to the institutions trying to find out what I could do. I asked the Committee in Munich, the American commander, everyone. One day I bumped into a friend of mine and he said, "Hershke, what's happening? You look confused." I told him my story and he said, "I know a mayor in a little town; let me talk to him and see what we can do." In a few days he came to see me and said the mayor had agreed to give us the license. We went to the town, had the ceremony with two witnesses, signed the papers, and we were ready. I began to breathe a little easier. There would be no more delays.

Our DP camp was closed and we were put into a bigger one in Landsberg. A couple of weeks after we were moved to that camp,

The DP Camp

my wife and I were called to the American Consulate. When we went for the FBI interrogation, a lot of people were waiting. When someone came out of the office, all the others wanted to know what they had been asked and whether they had made it hard for them. Sometimes in their nervousness, people gave the wrong answers, so they compared information with their records, and if you had made a mistake they would let you wait for a few weeks and would call you back. Many people weren't accepted the first time.

When it came my turn, my wife and I went in together. The whole interrogation took five minutes. The American told us that everything was in order and we left the room.

One week later we got a letter to go before the American doctors. I was scared that, God forbid, they would find something wrong with me. I had heard all kinds of stories that the American doctors were turning a lot of people away because of their health. The main thing they watched was the lungs. I was afraid they would find something with my lungs, since I may have had tuberculosis when I was in the hospital so long. Some people they told to wait and come back in a few months or a year, but others couldn't go the the United States at all. Uncle Borach did not get permission to emigrate because of his mental breakdown and TB.

Waiting in the doctor's office, we saw people who couldn't go to the United States because of their health run out of the office tearing their hair from their heads; some committed suicide, we heard later. We could hear the wailing when they were told. I was afraid, but I decided that what would be would be.

The day my wife and I appeared before the doctors, they took our blood pressure, checked for venereal disease, checked our eyes. This part we passed with no problem.They took x-rays of our lungs and told us to come back the next day. That night we couldn't sleep. As soon as it got light, we went to wait for the doctors. Even though they didn't come in until nine, we were there by six. Finally the doctor called out our names and we went into his office. He told us to sit down and said he had the results of the test. He was very friendly and talked to us in broken German. He asked us where we were going to try to settle. He took out the x-rays, very little ones like the ones they use for teeth, and put them under the light, and said that everything was okay. He wished us luck in the new land.

When we heard those words, we knew we were going to the United States. The only thing left to do was to appear before the consulate and be sworn in. After that, it was as good as done. We were so happy, so overjoyed, that in the next few weeks we would be in the most democratic country in the whole world. A few days later we were called to the consulate. With us was a Lithuanian interpreter. He told us to lift our hands and swear, and then the American signed our visas in red ink.

Every two weeks a ship left for the United States from Bremerhaven. At the camp there we went through one more interrogation by the FBI and a doctor's examination, but it was only a formality. On February 18, 1949, we left for the United States on a military boat, the SS *Marine Shark*.

32. The Voyage to the United States

We boarded the boat on a Monday evening. There were about three hundred DPs in all. The women were put on one floor and the men on the floor beneath them. On the top floor were the captain and crew. After assigning us to beds, we were taken to the dining area, where there were tables set up, and told to sit down and eat. The food was delicious. There were delicacies like grapefruit that I had never seen. I had to ask the waiter how to eat it.

We were supposed to leave the harbor that evening, but a dense fog delayed us until the next morning. The first three days were beautiful, like going on a cruise, until we left the English Channel, and then the boat started pitching. That evening, when we went into the dining room to eat, the tables and dishes were going up and down and a lot of dishes were broken.

We couldn't eat, so we went back to our bunks. Since the men were on the bottom floor, each wave hit the side of the boat next to us and we thought the boat was breaking open. The whole night I couldn't sleep for the bouncing. The next morning I crawled down from my bed to go to the deck for some fresh air, but the boat was still pitching. My head started spinning and I fell down. I crawled back to my bed. All my friends were seasick. A few who reached the deck never came back to the bottom; they just covered themselves and sat on the deck until we reached New York. For me the seasickness lasted three days. After that, I felt a little better. My wife was seasick for the whole fourteen days of the voyage.

Several times the captain had us put on our life jackets. Once a little girl ran up and started screaming, "The boat is sinking." A toilet on the women's floor had overflowed. That is the way it went until March 2. Because it was late, the ship anchored a few miles from the harbor. The moment the sick ones who had wanted to be thrown overboard heard that they would see New York the next day, their sickness disappeared. Everyone ran to his room and started shaving and getting dressed up so he would make a good impression on the family that would be waiting at the dock.

Genya and I got ready. We couldn't wait for the moment when we would meet my uncle. I didn't know what I would say to him. I remembered the clothes they used to send me when I was a child, very expensive things. All the DPs were nervous. We were running back and forth to the deck to see what we could. There were only a few searchlights.

The last night on the boat no one slept. At 6:00 AM small tugboats started pulling the ship into the harbor. All the passengers were on deck waiting to see New York. They took us past the Statue of Liberty. Everyone stood with large eyes and open mouths as we came close to the dock and saw before us huge skyscrapers. As the boat anchored and we started getting off, we could hear screaming and crying—this time, of happiness as families met. We were finally free from the shadow of death. Here we would begin our new lives.

33. The New Life

My uncle never met us. As Jean and I sat on the pier waiting for him we were surrounded by other passengers being met by their relatives and friends. Long hours passed. I began to feel anxious that Uncle Jack had not arrived. We waited into the evening. All the other DPs had left by then. I went to the Red Cross worker in charge and told her we were still waiting for my uncle. She took my name and my uncle's name and came back in five minutes with a message that Uncle Jack was unable to meet us but had sent some train tickets for us to travel to Bear Lake, Pennsylvania, where I was to work on his mink farm.

Jean started yelling at me, "How do we find a train? How do we find our way to Pennsylvania?" Neither one of us spoke English and we had only some pocket money. As I tried to calm her she suddenly remembered that she had an old aunt living somewhere in New York. With the help of the Red Cross worker, my wife found the telephone number and called her. After talking about fifteen minutes the aunt invited us to stay with her for a week. She gave us her address and told us to take a taxi; she would pay for it.

We went out to catch a taxi; it was about 7:30 PM. We saw not one taxi but hundreds of taxis—and buses, trucks, people running around as if they were insane. We managed to stop a taxi, and I tried to tell the driver—half in German, half in Yiddish, with my wife talking in Polish—where to take us as I showed him the paper with the address on it. We finally reached the aunt's house somewhere in Brooklyn. She was very nice. There were a lot of questions about my wife's family—where and how they had died.

During that week, we tried to get accustomed to the noise and the life of the city. We walked through the streets in Brooklyn trying to figure out what was happening. People seemed to swarm like flies. They didn't walk, they ran. Where was everyone running to?

After that, I went to work for Uncle Jack on the mink farm in Pennsylvania. But things didn't work out as I had expected. My mother's brothers did not have the kind of family feelings that I had grown up with in their father's house, with my aunts and uncles and cousins. In America it was each person for himself. In order to make a living I had to go back to New York, where Jean and I worked in the garment district until I was fired as a pawn in a union dispute.

We decided that New York was too big, and we applied to the Joint Distribution Committee, a Jewish relief organization, for resettlement. At that time, the only opening was in Madison, Wisconsin. The countryside in Wisconsin was not so different from that in Lithuania. The cities were smaller and more familiar. My wife and I had three children before we parted and went our separate ways. I became a scrap metal dealer, a junkman, traveling the back roads to farms, small towns, and factories—a Yiddish peddler who came back from the dead. But that's a story for another time.